RESEARCH HIGHLIGHTS IN SOCIAL WORK 40

Managing Front Line Practice in Social Work

Edited by Daphne Statham

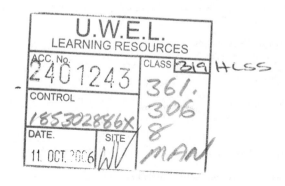

Jessica Kingsley Publishers
London and New York

First published in the United Kingdom in 2004
by Jessica Kingsley Publishers Ltd
116 Pentonville Road
London N1 9JB, England
and
29 West 35th Street, 10th fl.
New York, NY 10001-2299, USA
www.jkp.com

Copyright © Jessica Kingsley Publishers 2004

Library of Congress Cataloging in Publication Data
A CIP catalog record for this book is available from the Library of Congress

British Library Cataloguing in Publication Data
A CIP catalogue record for this book is available from the British Library

ISBN 1 84310 886 X

Printed and Bound in Great Britain by
Athenaeum Press, Gateshead, Tyne and Wear

RESEARCH HIGHLIGHTS IN SOCIAL WORK 40

Managing Front Line Practice in Social Care

Research Highlights in Social Work

This topical series examines areas of particular interest to those in social and community work and related fields. Each book draws together different aspects of the subject, highlighting relevant research and drawing out implications for policy and practice. The project is under the editorial direction of Professor Joyce Lishman, Head of the School of Applied Social Studies at the Robert Gordon University.

of related interest

Social Work and Evidence-Based Practice
Edited by David Smith
Research Highlights in Social Work 45
ISBN 1 84310 156 4

Adult Day Services and Social Inclusion
Better Days
Edited by Chris Clark
Research Highlights in Social Work 39
ISBN 1 85302 887 8

The Changing Role of Social Care
Edited by Bob Hudson
Research Highlights in Social Work 37
ISBN 1 85302 752 9

Risk Assessment in Social Care and Social Work
Edited by Phyllida Parsloe
Research Highlights in Social Work 36
ISBN 1 85302 689 1

Social Care and Housing
Edited by Ian Shaw, Susan Lambert and David Clapham
Research Highlights in Social Work 32
ISBN 1 85302 437 6

Reconceptualising Work with 'Carers'
New Directions for Policy and Practice
Edited by Kirsten Stalker
Research Highlights in Social Work 43
ISBN 1 84310 118 1

Women Who Offend
Edited by Gill McIvor
Research Highlights in Social Work 44
ISBN 1 84310 154 8

Contents

Figure and Table

CHAPTER 1

The Context for Managing Practice

Daphne Statham

Over the past ten years there has been a gradual realisation that there is an intimate relationship between the attention given to the management and development of practice and delivering services and practice that are valued by people using services. This recognition is not new within social work or other professions whose daily work brings them into contact with people who are facing distressing life experiences. Isobel Menzies Lyth (1988) in the 1970s identified that without support nurses used survival techniques to cope with patients' emotional and physical pain that reduced their involvement with patients. In the 1990s the Department of Health's research into child care found that experienced workers will not hear the child's pain if there is no legitimised time for the workers to recover from their own distress (Department of Health 1991). This was less well understood among policy makers and politicians than it is in the early twenty-first century. The requirement for supervision in social work is now embedded in the employers' code of practice produced by the general councils regulating social care in the different countries of the UK (CCW 2002, GSCC 2002, NICC 2002, SSSC 2002). Employers are required have written policies and procedures in place for 'Effectively managing and supervising staff to support effective practice and good conduct and supporting staff to address deficiencies in their performance'.

As part of this process the management of practice has moved from being a professional to a public space. The chapters in this book identify evidence that:

- the quality of a service is determined by the process and the values underpinning social care, not simply by what is provided (Turner and Evans, Chapter 3)

- supervision is part of the governance of the organisation when what happens at the front line becomes the focus of political scrutiny (Cunningham, Chapter 5)

- organisations are most likely to learn from their own practice when there is a culture where service users directly influence policy, practice development and training (Beresford, Croft and Wulff-Cochrane, Chapter 2)

- the first line manager is the arbiter of quality (Kearney, Chapter 6; Learner and Rosen, Chapter 7)

- safeguarding a black organisation's mission and remaining connected with local black communities creates the space for culturally competent practice and services and an organisation that can learn from its front line practice (Ejo, Chapter 4)

- the personal characteristics of the workforce and the context in which they are working are resources for developing good practice (Foster, Chapter 8).

Combined these factors have moved the management of practice from being the supervision of an individual's work to one of the mechanisms to measure the quality of the organisation's primary objective – support and services to people using services. With the establishment of a new infrastructure of regulation, standard setting and knowledge dissemination in social care, the management of practice is the concern not only of local and central government but also of regulatory organisations in the four countries of the UK. Part of their function is to remove the postcode lottery of what you get depends on where you live and whether you are 'lucky' enough to be allocated a 'good' social worker. This is irrespective of whether the organisation she or he works is large, medium or small, in the statutory, voluntary or private sector, or the worker is independent. These are uncharted waters.

We are in the process of changing the game not just the rules about the management and development of social work that will impact from the macro systems level to the micro level of the interactions between the social worker and people using services. National occupational standards, codes of practice and service standards explicitly give the wider public an interest in social work's detailed operations and the means for politicians, employers and people using services to hold us to account. The implications for the management of practice are profound.

- Social work will increasingly be a collective activity carried out in multidisciplinary and multiorganisational teams that involve people using services as members.

- Change that is rapid and can be described as 'hectic' will require attention to the past policies and expectations being part of the dynamic in teams and organisations.

- Service users and their organisations are active in defining what is good practice, services, and the content and delivery of qualifying training.

- Social work is being reconstructed to be fit for purpose in this new scenario.

- Social policies are directly structuring the content of practice as well as the broad context for practice.

Social work as a collective activity

Social work has often been seen as establishing a professional relationship to achieve an outcome between a worker and an individual service user and their social network. This is a misconception; it is almost always a team activity. Social workers routinely operate in many different types of teams, not just as a group of social workers and social care workers employed by the same organisation and located geographically together. It is equally likely that team members are drawn together to create a mix of skills from different organisations and sectors, with service users and members of their family or social network integral to the achievement of agreed outcomes. Clarity about what constitutes the team is not just semantic. Conceptions of who is, and who is not, part of the team are part of constructing the nature of the practice and what has to be managed. If a team is composed of whoever is necessary to achieve an agreed outcome (Smale *et al.* 2000), the establishment of trust between members becomes a crucial issue. Accurate recognition of who is a member of that team is likely to produce open communication and reduce the resentment that happens when people are excluded from decision making (Department of Health 2003).

An assumption of homogeneity among team members also provides a false basis for the management of practice. Even in the traditional idea of a social worker team, members will have been trained at different times. Given the past battleground about the purpose and theory base of social work, at least some of these differences will be reflected in the team, with some members reverting to outdated theories and attitudes when under pressure (Lauerman 1997). Receptionists, administrators and secretaries routinely interface with the public and are part of the team's culture. In mixed skill and multiorganisational teams there are, in addition, different status, values and cultures, pay and conditions of service. A multiprofessional team will be working to different codes of practice and priorities that are likely to be more firmly embedded in their work than the newer service frameworks that cross professional and organisational boundaries. These issues are part of managing practice whether they relate to individual workers or are inherent in the organisation's culture. As Marsh and Fisher (1992) point out, 'the way it is done here' is a powerful force in shaping front line practice.

The leadership task for team managers is to use their understanding of these pasts and presents to develop the practice of the organisation as well as its individual members. Knowledge of history and heritage is part of the toolkit of the manager. It is an integral part of the task of working with the combustible mix of individual team members' value bases and theoretical frameworks, changing membership, the culture of the organisations we work in and with. This understanding enables the manager to direct energies and skills towards the collective effort to provide quality services and practice. This history affects us all and conceptions about the management of practice.

Identifying the past in our present as a task for the management of practice

The methods used to refocus the social work task in the 1970s and 1980s were a plethora of procedures and guidance to limit professional judgement. Not confined to social work, the policy trend held professionals as well as managers accountable for the efficiency and effectiveness of the organisation. Social work was equated with promoting dependency on state provision and a refusal to accept a mixed economy of care. The low regard for what social work could achieve and, in some places, a view that it was pernicious, had a profound effect on the management of practice. Tasks became more circumscribed around assessments and areas of high risk such as child abuse and the protection of vulnerable adults. Workers were required to focus down on grading personal problems according to levels of eligibility based on the individual's dependence or vulnerability. The management of practice in many local authorities focused on the rationing of resources – the worker's time, services and finances – and procedures. Whatever the intention of these policies their effect was to force service users to demonstrate weaknesses, not strengths, and to constrict the development of social work.

The unpopularity of the word 'poverty' deliberately refocused practice away from attention to low incomes, poor health, housing, education and unemployment and their effects on people's life chances. The development of practice as part of the management task almost disappeared in many statutory organisations alongside preventative work. It survived in the voluntary sector and in therapeutic centres. During this period many social workers had 'almost to smuggle in their skills' (Platt 1998), while their employers concentrated on assessments of eligibility and the rationing of services and time. Social work became a rarity in many organisations. The historian E.P. Thompson (unpublished) once said that a movement for social change takes about twenty years. If he was right the management of practice has to accept that the impact of these past policies are still embedded in the way our organisations operate, in the frameworks practitioners are accustomed to using. These can override the newer policy imperatives in smaller or greater ways. The consistency of the research on the views of service users about the failure of social workers to listen, to show respect, to value their own culture, expertise and experience is evidence that there is still far to go in tackling this heritage.

The service user and liberation movements

The service user movement played a major part in the struggle to address these deficits in practice. The emphasis on the consumer, their rights and choices (Griffiths 1988) mitigated the political shift towards social work becoming a more technical task and created a climate in which the voices of people using services were heard by government. There was no lack of evidence. Bandana Ahmad (1990), Begum and Gillespie-Sells (1993; 1996) Suzy Croft and Peter Beresford (1990), Jane Campbell (1996), Peter Campbell (1990), Viv Lindow (1994), Jenny Morris (1993; 1994), Mike Oliver (1983), People First (1994) and Values into Action (1995) were among the writers and researchers producing theoretical insights as well as practical information on services and practice that promoted the independence and autonomy of service users. In 1995 service users were involved for the first time in the development of practice. *The Services We Expect ...* (Harding and Beresford 1996) drew together these views to contribute to the development of National Occupational Standards for social work. The REU (formerly the Race Equality Unit) produced a steady stream of evidence on the impact of racism on services and practice throughout the 1990s and guidance to improve practice (Butt 1994; Butt and Mirza 1996, Butt and Box 1997). Gender issues were also well researched. The 1980s saw books by Jo Campling (1981) on disabled women, Pat Carlen and Anne Worrall (1987) on women and criminal justice, Angela Coyle (1984) on unemployment, Rebecca and Russell Dobash (1980) on domestic violence, Naomi Gottleib and colleagues (1980), Jalna Hanmer and Daphne Statham (1988) and Lena Dominelli and Eileen McLeod (1989) on social work with women.

These perspectives struggled with social work theories permeated with a view that the professional was the expert in solving other people's problems rather than an expert in problem solving (Smale *et al.* 2000). In addition to a heavy emphasis on money and procedures there was lack of agreement about the role of social work and an absence of mechanisms that could negotiate a way through conflicting perspectives or any political will to create them. Inevitably the management of practice suffered in many organisations. It continued to thrive where confident first line managers safeguarded the time and space for the development of practice. They in turn were often protected by people in the hierarchy who were committed to social work as a resource for promoting community well-being. The policy focus on user-centred services and outcomes still has not made sufficient inroads to change the status of the management of practice in relation to other forms of management. Yet responsive and reflective practice demands high levels of intellectual and professional skills.

The evidence from organisations controlled by people using services was that the relationship – the personal skills and attitudes of the workers – gave a service its quality. A high value was placed on the capacity of the worker to listen, to respect the person and their experience and expertise, and to spend time listening, providing information and working through options. This focus on basic social work skills created the possibility of alliances at the local, national and political level on the reconstruction of the role of social care and, within it, of social work. This was facilitated by a consistency across the different government administrations about the responsibility of health and social care to achieve outcomes valued by people using these services rather than professionals deciding what is good for them. As always there are inconsistencies between the policies. In mental health, criminal justice and work with asylum seekers the balance is tipped towards control and public protection, but even here there is a sense that engaging people in exploring options that they value is more likely to achieve change, even if at times it becomes submerged.

Social constructions of social work

For the first time there is an international definition of social work. A press release produced by the International Association of Schools of Social Work and the International Federation of Social Workers in 2002 (p.I) it states that social work is:

a profession which promotes social change, problem solving in human re-lationships and the empowerment and liberation of people to enhance well being. Utilising theories of human behaviour and social systems, social work intervenes at the points where people interact with their envi-ronments. Principles of human rights and social justice are fundamental to social work.

Although social work has these enduring features all over the world, context has a profound effect. Governments, history and cultures have a key role in shaping how social work operates and what expertise is given priority. Particular constructions of social work respond to social and economic conditions, changes in demography and political conceptions of what creates or will restore the 'good society'. In extreme cases what is legitimate can change almost overnight. One of the starkest examples was in Chile under Allende's socialist government in the 1970s. Chilean social workers were responsible for community development, but after the military coup led by Colonel Pinochet this was a criminal act.

If social work practice is socially constructed it can also be recon-structed, and expectations of its management will also change. Remnants of past reconstructions in the UK persist over time in parts of our organisations and in the memories of past and present service users. In spite of some twenty years of promoting the idea that service users are citizens with rights and re-sponsibilities there are persistent reports in research of the paternalism experienced by service users and a failure to listen and respect their views (Beresford and Turner 1997), to address ethnicity, cultural and spiritual re-quirements (Butt and Mirza 1996; Department of Health 2000a; Ejo, Chapter 4).

In the late 1990s and the early 2000s social work's role in the modernising agenda for health, education, housing, income support and local government has begun to locate it in mainstream services instead of as a resource only for those who fail (Social Services Inspectorate 1999). Service users retain their citizenship, their rights and responsibilities, under human rights legislation except where these are removed or limited by law.

Identifying the social work role in implementing key social

There are four social policy themes that impact directly on shaping practice and its management. These are:

1. the social model

2. the well-being or public health agenda

3. social regeneration and capacity building

4. the knowledge economy.

While opinions on solutions may differ, there is a consensus among the political parties that these elements are crucial to social and, more importantly in political terms, economic policies.

The social model

The social model, developed by disabled people, identifies the barriers created for disabled people by attitudes and behaviour, the environment, organisations and structures. It is used widely throughout social care to refocus practice on outcomes that people using services want. Black and minority ethnic groups tend to use the term 'holistic' and others 'ecological', but there are common elements between them. Each requires practitioners to routinely look for resources beyond their own narrow remit and to see the person in their complexity, with expertise and experience and a social network, rather than as a problem. The term 'holistic' is scattered liberally throughout the literature and is increasingly equated with quality. Holistic practice is described as best practice in the annual report of the Chief Inspector of Social Services in England (Department of Health 2000b) and as being found in workers who:

> have developed the skills and judgement to assess and gain a better under-
> standing of a person in the context of their family, their environment and
> the social circumstances, and they ensure that they respond to these needs
> flexibly. They have the skills to gain access to a range of community and
> other resources and to allocate them on the basis of individual or family
> need. They routinely consult the people who use the services, and their
> carers, and involve them in planning their care. They are committed to im-

proving the well being of the communities they serve and to promoting social inclusion. (p.7)

The social model has a number of implications for the management of practice. First, it places the service user, their expertise and experience at the centre rather than the worker or the organisation(s) involved. Its ultimate expression is direct payments where, after determining eligibility, the power to decide who and what is provided is in the hands of the disabled person and not those of the worker or the service. Second, teamwork is high priority, as is creating teams with mixed skills and expertise who between them can operate through direct and indirect practice to tackle social problems at the community as well as at the individual and family level (Smale *et al.* 2000). Kearney, Levin and Rosen's (2000) research shows social workers contributing in these multi disciplinary and multiorganisational teams by problem spotting and solving at the boundaries between organisations and people. The model helps to ensure that the particular area of expertise of the worker does not determine the response to disabled children from black and minority ethnic communities by focusing on their impairment and neglecting their identity and cultural and religious needs (Amad *et al.* 1998).

The social model is seen as crucial in moving the focus of practice towards outcomes. Nicholas, Quereshi and Bamford (2003) argue that the social model is the means by which:

- the focus can be held on what people using services prefer
- recognition can be given to the fact that people have different perspectives on the outcomes that they want to achieve and that these differences have to be treated as equally valid
- it is ensured that explanations are given for the reasons one particular outcome is chosen
- the attention is directed towards other services and resources that are important to the service user but are outside the remit of the practitioner and their managers.

The social model often places social work at the edge – or on the margins – rather than in the centre of the action. Remaining marginal is highly skilful (Smale *et al.* 2000). The worker has to keep hold of different and sometimes conflicting views and perspectives to retain an overview of the context and to understand the specific expertise and resources required to deliver a particular outcome. The position prioritises skills in negotiation, networking, creativity in the face of limited resources and facilitating the empowerment of the people using services and key individuals in their social network. The idea that a team is made up of whoever is needed to accomplish the task (Smale *et al.* 2000) is the foundation for implementing the social model and multiprofessional and multiorganisational work.

The well-being agenda

The well-being agenda (Department of Health 1999) sees poverty, unemployment, poor educational achievement, housing and poor health interacting in complex ways to reduce life opportunities for individuals and families. The end result is that the key government department is not necessarily the Department of Health. Policies for housing recognise the impact housing can have on both the social and health well-being of individuals and families (Department of the Environment, Transport and the Regions 2000) and Best Value Indicators intersect with education and health (Office of the Deputy Prime Minister 2003) as does Quality Protects (Department of Health 1998). Managers of practice have to scan these horizons and to have the capacity to locate the contribution that social work can make within these wider frameworks.

The well-being agenda, or in local authority terms the responsibility to promote the economic, social and environmental well-being of communities, provides a framework within which social work can flourish because it is consistent with a holistic and social model. The features they share in common are:

- economic, social and environmental factors are seen to have an impact on life chances
- the person, family or group is seen within their social support system and their communities
- locality, culture and history are recognised and valued as part of the solution

- the focus is on outcomes valued by people using services and local communities.

The means to achieve this are not only through partnerships between health, social care, housing and education services but also through building up social cohesion and the capacity of local people and organisations to become active in tackling issues. Regaining and enhancing citizen participation in education, voluntary work and employment provides health gains as well as the social capital that these activities create (Davies 2001). The creative social work role of marginality is crucial to tailoring these interventions.

Social regeneration and capacity building

This agenda flows from and localises the well-being framework by investing in local people and communities. It recognises that empowerment can only be facilitated, not given to people, and that outsiders' priorities are often not those of insiders. There is consistent evidence that the black and minority ethnic voluntary sector is judged to provide appropriate and effective services where mainstream services fail to achieve this (Butt and Mirza 1997). Investments in areas that have not involved people living there in decision making have all too often not brought sustained improvements in deprived and run-down areas. Similarly, initiatives developed by local organisations and interest groups, although poorly resourced, can have a greater impact locally (Social Exclusion Unit 1998).

Partnerships between local people and organisations can be very effective in making neighbourhoods safer, in resolving conflicts between the younger and older generation, and encouraging skills development and the gaining of qualifications that have enabled people to get jobs and become involved. Social work needs to articulate its contribution to promoting social regeneration and to reclaim some of the substantial body of expertise and theory on community development that existed in the 1960s and 1970s.

The awareness of differences in power between different groups working in partnerships and of negotiating the impact of these, identifying and working with conflicts, accessing information and enabling people to develop their knowledge and skills are all key to social work. Without this knowledge and capacity the equality in partnerships can be a lost cause. Marjorie Mayo and Marilyn Taylor (2001) explore how this lack of understanding can subvert effective joint action in the regeneration programmes they reviewed. Community representatives voiced common concerns: they thought they were 'saddled with outputs that exclude community concerns' or 'It's about someone else's agenda. They just want you to tinker with this bit or that bit. You are never actually asked to set the priorities'. The best of social work could have ensured that some of these points were addressed. In addition, the awareness of discrimination and culture can ensure that black and minority ethnic groups are properly involved in setting the agenda as well as the outputs and outcomes they value. The success of community re-generation and capacity building is to be found in the degree that the people who use services are involved in community partnerships, since they are most likely to be among the most socially excluded in the area. Alliances with them to promote education, health and safer communities all require attention to processing and providing both technical support and training tailored to their needs to overcome these obstacles to participation (Mayo and Taylor 2001). A narrow social care focus neglects the key part that mainstream services such as transport, housing, adequate heating and accessible environments have on people's lives.

The knowledge-based practice and the learning organisation

We are in an era when promoting access to knowledge once limited to professionals is becoming widespread as a matter of policy. This is not just about information and communication technology or the requirement for continuing professional development; it is also about communicating and structuring knowledge so that it ceases to be exclusive to the few. While many people using services remain information poor, a growing number will have access to information through local groups, advocates and user-led organisations. Professional expertise now includes the capacity to communicate complex information in language that is accessible and enabling people to access information themselves. The boundaries between what is professional and what is lay knowledge are being redrawn. The implication for the manager is that she or he needs to:

- know how to access the information that underpins good practice, where knowledge is weak or absent

- relate this directly to the work of the practitioner as part of the traditional role of supervision in directing, and supporting the development of, practice

- understand how people learn and how to audit the team's knowledge and that of individuals within the team to identify and access resources for their continuing learning

- enable practitioners to communicate their knowledge to individuals using services and their social network and to access knowledge directly

- contribute to the learning organisation by structuring front-line information as a resource for the development of the organisation's policies, practice, provision and commissioning.

These tasks are carried out in a context where knowledge is drawn from different perspectives. The service user movement talks not about knowledge but about knowledges, because knowledge can be structured in different ways (Croft, Beresford and Wulff-Cochrane, Chapter 2). Failure to recognise this important distinction can lead us to assume that consensus is present when none exists. The women's, black and gay liberation movements, in their struggles to restructure knowledge, clearly demonstrated the way that questions can be framed to exclude their perspective and experience and to ensure that the information that emerged that would not challenge existing ways of seeing the world.

The Social Care Institute for Excellence and it medical equivalent, the National Institute for Clinical Excellence, give us a more structured way of negotiating with the stakeholders how the different knowledges can contribute to improving practice outcomes for people using services. They will provide a means by which we can surface and expunge outdated theories and guidance through the management of practice. Equally significant is that the knowledge – or the lack of it – on which we base our judgements will become open, explicit and challengeable.

Basic to practice management are skills in accessing information and in communicating it to workers in ways that support their work and model the expertise they will need to acquire to do the same for people using services. These skills are an essential element of accountability to people using services and to the governance of the organisation itself. All social workers should develop a skill in conveying information about the knowledge basis underpinning the assessments and decisions made about people that frequently affect the detail of their daily lives, and sometimes their liberties and their rights as individuals and parents.

The boundaries between different professional knowledges are also being redrawn, and consequently the areas of our shared knowledge will become greater and our specific knowledge more precise. For example, social care and medicine deal routinely with managing risk. The summary of the implications from a recent research programme on communicating risks in public health is familiar territory for social work. It was found that effective communication was promoted when there was clarification of areas of disagreement and support for people to make more considered decisions, that involving people avoided resentment about exclusion that blocked collective working, that the source of the information needs to be trusted, and that nonverbal messages are as important as the verbal message. These are familiar lessons in social work – though not always practiced by us. The report adds that playing the 'I am the expert' game does not necessarily gain trust, which is most likely to be created by openness and being ready to listen (Department of Health 2003). There are also similar findings in work on violence to social care staff where the task force worked closely with the Royal College of Psychiatry (Lindow and McGeorge 2001). The National Service Frameworks are structured to enable multidisciplinary and multiagency working. This eases the capacity to work across professional and organisational boundaries but places additional demands on managers of practice to stay up to date within their field and across the boundaries connected to it. While success used to be staying firmly within the profession, it is now found to be in working at and across the margins.

The reconstruction of social work and the mechanisms for its development have determined the structure for this book. It begins with chapters on the management of practice written by people using services before it moves to exploring the management of practice.

Chapter 2 uses work undertaken over two years that brought people using services, practitioners, policy makers and managers to consider what social work will look like in the future.

Chapter 3 continues this theme by drawing on research the authors have undertaken on what people using services value from social work and social care. The work demonstrated that there were considerable areas of agreement about the direction social work should be taking.

Chapter 4 uses research on the development of the Bibini Centre for black children and young people. To create culturally competent services the management of practice has to address the context of the lives of the young people, their families, the workers, the attitudes and behaviour of other or-ganisations towards black organisations, and the people who use their services.

Chapter 5 reviews research on what needs to be in place to enable good practice to flourish. The features identified are individual and team supervision to capture collective expertise; using available knowledge to underpin assessments and decision making; combining external standards, statutory and organisational requirements and procedures.

Chapter 6 outlines the work in the Ulster Community and Health Trust over a period of seven years to improve practice and contribute to social care governance. Research and literature on social work supervision was used to enable supervision to contribute directly to quality assurance and governance within the trust.

Chapter 7 describes the work the authors undertook in social services departments where standards had fallen below acceptable levels. The focus is on duty or assessment and referral teams in children's services which are the doorway to services and the first contact for people using services, and often for professionals as well, setting the tone for future relationships.

Chapter 8 considers the role of gender in the management of practice and argues that supervision is concerned with the quartet of the service user, the carer, the practitioner and the first line manager. The gender structure of the workforce and the social context in which the quartet operates, the gendered nature of the problems women bring to social workers and the impact of gender on management styles are examined.

Chapter 9 notes the lack of research on the management of practice and brings together the research issues raised by this collection of papers which should be addressed as part of using the management of practice to promote continuing professional development and practice improvement.

References

Ahmad, B. (1990) *Black Perspectives in Social Work.* Birmingham: Venture Press.

Ahmad, W., Darr, A., Jones, L. and Nisar, G. (1998) *Deafness and Ethnicity: Services, Policy and Politics.* Bristol: Policy Press.

Association of Directors of Social Service and the National Institute for Social Work (1997) *Managing Contradiction and Avoidance.* London: National Institute for Social Work.

Begum, N. and Gillespie-Sells, K. (1993) *Towards Managing User Led Services.* London: Race Equality Unit.

Beresford, P. and Croft, S. (1993) *Citizen Involvement: A Practical Guide for Change.* Basingstoke: Macmillan.

Beresford, P. and Turner, M. (1997) *It's Our Welfare: Report of the Citizen's Commission on the Future of Welfare.* London: National Institute for Social Work.

Butt, J. (1994) *Same Service or Equal Service? The Second Report on Social Services Departments' Implementation and Monitoring of Services for Black and Ethnic Minority Communities.* London: HMSO.

Butt, J., Box, L. and Lyn Cook, S. (1999) *Respect, Learning Materials for Social Care Staff Working with Black and Minority Ethnic Older People.* London: REU (formerly the Race Equality Unit).

Butt, J. and Mirza, K. (1996) *Supportive Services; Effective Strategies.* London: REU (formerly the Race Equality Unit).

Campbell, J. and Oliver, M. (1996) *Disability Politics: Understanding our Pasts, Changing Our Futures.* London: Routledge.

Campbell, P. (1990) 'Mental Health Self-Advocacy.' In L. Winn (ed) *Power to the People.* London: Kings Fund Centre.

Campling, J. (1981) *Images of Ourselves: Women with Disabilities.* London: Routledge Kegan Paul.

Carlen, P. and Worrall, A. (eds) (1987) *Gender, Crime and Justice.* Milton Keynes: Open University Press.

CCW (Care Council for Wales) (2002) *Codes of Practice for Social Care Workers and Employers.* Cardiff: CCW.

Croft, S. and Beresford, P. (1990) *From Paternalism to Participation: Involving People in Social Services.* London: Open Services Project.

Coyle, A. (1984) *Redundant Women.* London: Women's Press.

Davies, J.K. (2001) 'Partnership Working in Health Promotion: The Potential Role of Social Capital in Health Development.' In S. Balloch and M. Taylor (eds) *Partnership Working: Policy and Practice.* Bristol: Policy Press.

Department of the Environment, Transport and the Regions (2000) *Joining it Up Locally, National Strategy for Neighbourhood Renewal.* Report of Policy Action Team 17. London: Stationery Office.

Department of Health (1991) *Patterns and Outcomes in Child Placement.* London: HMSO.

Department of Health (1998) *Quality Protects Circular: Transforming Children's Services.* Local Authority Circular, (Lac (98) 28)

Department of Health (1999) *Reducing Inequalities: An action report of the Department of Health.* London: Department of Health.

Department of Health (2000a) *Excellence and Not Excuses.* London: Social Services Inspectorate.

Department of Health (2000b) *Modern Social Services: A Commitment to People: The Ninth Annual Report of the Chief Inspector of Social Services 1999–2000.* London: The Stationery Office.

Department of Health (2001) *Learning from Bristol: the Department of Health Response to the Report of the Public Inquiry into Children's Heart Surgery at the Bristol Royal Infirmary, 1984–1995.* London: Stationery Office.

Department of Health (2003) *Communicating About Risks To Public Health.* London: The Stationery Office. www.doh.gov.uk/pointers.htm

Dobash, R.E. and Dobash, R. (1980) *Violence Against Wives: A Case against Patriarchy.* Shepton Mallet: Open Books.

Dominelli, L. and McCleod, E. (1989) *Feminist Social Work.* London: Macmillan.

Gottleib, N. (ed) (1980) *Alternative Social Services for Women.* New York: Columbia University Press.

Griffiths, R. (1988) *Community Care: An Agenda for Action.* London: HMSO.

GSCC (General Social Care Council) (2002) *Codes of Practice for Social Care Workers and Employers.* London: GSCC.

Hanmer, J. and Statham, D. (1988) *Women and Social Work, Towards a Woman Centred Practice.* Basingstoke: Macmillan.

Harding, T. and Beresford, P. (1997) *The Services We Expect...* London: National Institute for Social Work.

International Association of Schools of Social Work and International Federation of Social Workers (2000) Press release on the International Definition of Social Work, July.

Jones, A. and Butt, J. (1995) *Taking the Initiative.* London: NSPCC.

Kearney, P., Levin, E. and Rosen, G. (2000) *Alcohol, Drugs and Mental Health Problems: Working with Families.* London: National Institute for Social Work.

Lindow, V. (1994) *Self Help and Alternatives.* London: Mental Health Foundation.

Lindow, V. and McGeorge, M. (2001) *Research on Violence Against Staff in Mental Health Inpatient and Community Settings.* London: Stationery Office.

Marsh, P. and Fisher, M. (1992) *Good Intentions: Developing Partnerships in Social Services.* York: Joseph Rowntree Foundation.

Mayo, M. and Taylor, M. (2001) 'Partnerships and Power in Community Regeneration.' In S. Balloch and M. Taylor (eds) *Partnership Working: Policy and Practice.* Bristol: Policy Press.

Menzies Lyth, I. (1988) 'The Functioning of Social Defence Mechanisms as a Defence Against Anxiety.' In *Containing Anxiety in Institutions, Selected Essays; Volume I.* London: Free Association Books.

Morris, J. (1993) *Disabled Live: Many Voices, One Message.* York: Joseph Rowntree Foundation.

Morris, J. (1994) *The Shape of Things to Come: User Led Services.* London: National Institute for Social Work.

Nicholas, E., Quereshi, H. and Bamford, C. (2003) *Outcomes into Practice: Focusing Practice and Information on the Outcomes for People. A Resource Pack.* York: Social Policy Research Unit, University of York.

NICC (Northern Ireland Care Council) (2002) *Codes of Practice for Social Care Workers and Employers.* Belfast: NICC.

Office of the Deputy Prime Minister (2003) *Best Value Performance Indicators 2003–4.* London: The Stationery Office.

Oliver, M. (1983) *Social Work with Disabled People.* Basingstoke: Macmillan.

People First (1994) *Oi! It's My First Assessment: Everything You Ever Wanted to Know about Community Care but Nobody Bothered To Tell You About.* London: Royal College of Psychiatrists.

Platt, D. (1998) 'Changing the role of social work.' Paper presented at the National Debate on the Future of Social Work conference. London, 23 September.

Smale, G., Tuson, G. and Statham, D. (2000) *Social Work and Social Problems.* Basingstoke: Macmillan.

Social Exclusion Unit (1998) *Bringing Britain Together: A National Strategy for Neighbourhood Renewal, Cm 4045.* London: The Stationery Office.

Social Exclusion Unit (2001) *National Strategy for Neighbourhood Renewal: A Framework for Consultation.* London: The Stationery Office.

SSSC (Scottish Social Services Council) (2002) *Codes of Practice for Social Care Workers and Employers.* Edinburgh: SSSC.

Task Force on Violence Towards Social Care Staff (2000) *A Safer Place.* www.doh.gov.uk/violencetaskforce

Thompson, E.P. (1987) Unpublished paper given at Ruskin College, Oxford Summer School for Trade Unionists.

CHAPTER 2

The Future of Social Work

Suzy Croft, Peter Beresford and Elizabeth Wulff-Cochrane

There is little use examining the management of social work practice without giving some thought to what the future shape of social work and social care is likely to be. This chapter is concerned with the future of social work and social care and particularly with the role that social work practitioners may play in shaping this. It draws on a series of conferences, seminars and presentations jointly organised by the National Institute for Social Work, the Centre for Citizen Participation, Brunel University, St John's Hospice, London, the Central Council for Education and Training in Social Work (CCETSW), *Community Care* magazine and Shaping Our Lives (SOL), which is a network of service-user-controlled organisations. All of these activities involved current social work practitioners (most also involved health and social care service users) fully and centrally. We use the term 'social work practitioners' to mean people whose work is centrally and mainly concerned with working with and having face-to-face contact with service users.

Marginalising practitioners

This combination of organisations is in itself unusual – as is the focus of this chapter. Current practitioners have played little part in shaping modern social work policy and practice or indeed in formal and official discussions about it. Practitioners have been marginal to the production of formal social work knowledge. While there has been no systematic study of this issue (another measure perhaps of the lack of priority attached to it), it is reflected in all areas of social work activity and development. Few government or other official social work committees include current social work practitioners, although their involvement in the reform of social work in 2001–02 is welcome. Pick up any textbook about child protection or indeed most other areas of social work. You will find few contributions from current practitioners. Managers, academics, policy makers and politicians are the key players and if they have direct experience as social work practitioners, this tends to be brief, long ago and far away from current situations.

For some this may not seem problematic. It might be argued that social work is too important to be left to social workers. Perhaps, but we are not arguing here against the involvement of other stakeholders. Far from it. We are particularly committed to the equal involvement of service users in the definition, development and undertaking of social work and for this reason this chapter is followed by Michael Turner's and Clare Evans's chapter on service users' influence on the development of policy, provision, practice and management.

What concerns us is the systematic and large-scale exclusion of practising social workers from the construction and development of social work. There are practical, philosophical and political arguments for including social work practitioners on equal terms in the social work project. First, what does it say about the profession's own valuing of social work practice if practitioners are not centrally involved in shaping it? Second, how can we expect practice to be 'fit for purpose' if it is not fully informed by practitioner knowledge and experience? Finally, what hope is there long term to improve the recruitment and retention of social work practitioners so long as they are treated as 'foot soldiers' who are merely expected 'to do or die' rather than 'reason why'?

Our concerns about the involvement of social work practitioners in the future of social work follow from our own perspectives. We write as a current social work practitioner, placement supervisor, service user, social work teacher and education and training manager. We believe that our roles have highlighted for us the importance of the contributions and insights of social work practitioners.

Time for change

This is an important time to be looking at the future of social work and considering the role of practitioners in it. We are at a period of major change and re-evaluation. Social work is now at one of the most vulnerable times in its history. In some ways, the phrase 'social work' has been written out of public policy. Important social work institutions like the National Institute for Social Work and the Central Council for Education and Training in Social Work now no longer exist. Instead we have organisations to regulate and set standards for practice and services in each of the countries of the UK, skills councils to develop training strategies and occupational standards for the social care workforce. In addition there are mechanisms for setting standards that cross the traditional boundaries between social care, health and education. There is now a Social Care Institute for Excellence (SCIE) and the Electronic Library for Social Care (eLSC) and the research web in Scotland. Social work education and training and their funding are undergoing radical reform. The Government has aimed for 'integration' between health and social care, with large new trusts linked with the radical reform of the National Health Service (NHS). Beyond this, social work and social care operate in the legislative context of the Disability Rights Commission, the extended Disability Discrimination Act, the Human Rights Act, the Race Relations (Amendment) Act 2000 (Home Office 2001) and mandatory provisions for direct payments enabling people to control their arrangements for support and personal assistance.

But social work's future must also be considered in the context of the tragic circumstances of the murder of Victoria Climbié in 2001 which triggered a major review not only of the capacity of social services departments to protect children, but of social work's contribution to child protection. The history of social work and personal social services for more than fifty years since the Second World War has been punctuated and seriously affected by a series of high-profile child care and child protection tragedies. These have exerted a far more important influence on the direction of policy and practice in social work than the equivalents in other areas of public policy, including medicine (Kennedy Report 2001; Department of Health 2002) have ever done. In the wake of Victoria Climbié's death and the Laming inquiry, there is again a strong sense that 'something must be done'. The actual impact this has on social work and social care, the form it takes, whether the effects will be for good or bad, remain unclear. Certainly it is another reason for seeking to ensure that social work's knowledge base is based on as firm foundations as possible – and that these routinely include the diversity of experience, knowledge and perspectives of social work practitioners. Between 1997 and 2001 we tried to address this gap by bringing together social work practitioners and service users to debate and record their views on future trends. The results of this work have fed into the development of the National Occupational Standards for Social Work (TOPSS 2002).

The National Debate on the Future of Social Work held in 1998 was the first national initiative to bring together social work practitioners and service users (NISW 1999). It was followed by events bringing practitioners from different parts of the UK to explore the future of social work (NISW 2000; Social Work 2000) and organised by services users to explore user involvement in social work education and training (SUET). The National Debate marked a formal beginning to a process of seeking to reconceive social work from the workers' and users' perspectives. There was a strong sense at this event that social work needed to be radically reconceived and restructured if it was to be relevant in a multi-ethnic society experiencing radical political, economic, social and cultural change. This activity, participants felt, had to be a joint and equal venture between people who used services and their workers.

While some differences emerged between service users and practitioners, there were many areas of agreement between them. This has also emerged in other initiatives bringing together their different perspectives (for example, Beresford and Trevillion 1995). As one debate participant said, 'I think social work is largely afraid of consulting service users because it is afraid of criticism. I think if they listen to research and listen to service users, they will find a lot of information that says why social work should be done, why it is important'.

A basis for shaping social work's future

Participants in the National Debate and the Social Work 2000 seminar identified a number of key principles, which they thought social work would need to build on for the future. These included:

- recognising different perspectives and balances of power, for example, between service users and service workers, for black and minority ethnic groups. One participant at the National Debate got strong support when she said: 'If we are looking at the future of social work and at redesigning it, then I would make a plea, that whatever the future is, it takes on board the wishes and needs of black people. The present is one where black people have been discriminated against in all areas of social care'

- demonstrating an understanding that individuals, groups and communities have equal rights, but sometimes different requirements and preferences and that these need appropriate and individual, rather than standardised, responses

- adopting an holistic approach to support which recognises the multidimensional nature and complex identity of people rather than building responses narrowly around traditional divisions such as impairment, ethnic origin, age, and so on

- commitment to the belief that everyone is capable of expressing their views and preferences, whatever the nature of their impairment, form of communication or disempowerment because of poverty or institutionalisation. A central role for social work is to identify the barriers and seek ways round them

- a return to social work as an activity concerned with fostering collective action as well as working on an individual basis to support individual empowerment and to support self-advocacy

- multidisciplinary analysis and multidisciplinary working: for example, recognising that housing, money, transport and accessible environments and practices are important for older and disabled people; that a black young person needs consideration to be given to identity, education, health and housing

- providing appropriate support early and not just when things have deteriorated or reached a crisis

- support for social workers to develop their practice, for practice to be valued and for routes to promotion within practice to be established; and last, but certainly not least

- prioritising social models based on rights, including:

  - human rights

  - rights based on legislation and guidance

  - agreed standards of practice and conduct

  - the concept of support and not 'care'.

As one service user said at the National Debate, 'We don't want care, we want rights. We want to change the nature of our relationship with social services and social work from one based on welfare to one based on social justice'.

It is worth expanding on this last principle, regarding social models. Social models place service users' experiences and knowledges in the centre of analysis of issues, problems and solutions whether the focus is on social support or social control. They have much in common with the holistic model developed by black people and minority ethnic groups. Both provide the foundations from which new forms of provision are being created by user-controlled organisations. Social work since the early 1990s has been using these frameworks to reshape its knowledge and its practice, so that it promotes independence and services tailored specifically to individuals and their support networks. The social model of disability was developed from the experience and expertise of disabled people (Oliver 1983). A social model of deafness has similarly been built from the experience of deaf communities. Mental health service users/survivors are also now exploring a social model of madness and distress (Beresford 2002). Social model approaches are now being developed to provide a broad framework which addresses the (similar and different) issues faced by mental health service users, older people, people with learning difficulties and people from black and minority ethnic groups. This work means that the social model is being developed to address diversity and difference between service users without losing what issues and concerns they share.

The social model of disability has also been the philosophy underpinning the independent living movement established by disabled people. This has been associated with the development of direct payment schemes putting the provision of support and personal assistance under the direct control of disabled people themselves. In 2002 it became mandatory for local services to offer direct payment schemes, and these are now coming to be used by a widening range of health and social care service users including people with physical and sensory impairments, mental health service users, young and older people, people with learning difficulties, people living with HIV/AIDS and black and minority ethnic service users. They have major implications for social work practitioners who are involved in the process of assessment to help service users to access direct payments. Social work practitioners will need to develop new skills and understanding to support service users to gain full and equal access to direct payments. This is becoming a new and increasingly important part of their role.

Social work values and skills

In the past the value base of social work has tended to be developed in an exclusive way. Practice that seeks to be emancipatory and liberating needs a value base that is shared between practitioners and service users. An approach, jointly developed and based on an inclusive framework of citizenship and human rights, offers this possibility. Social work practitioners and service users who came together in the Debate on the Future of Social Work prioritised values and skills which were user centred and focused on supporting service users to live their lives as positively as possible in the wider social world and to be able to negotiate the wider welfare service system with minimum harm and maximum benefit and support.

They also highlighted the importance of personal qualities in social workers as well as acquired skills, something that service users have emphasised whenever they have been asked what qualities they want from service workers but rarely raised in discussion within professional circles (Harding and Beresford 1996). Participants in the debate felt that social workers needed skills and values that support service users to empower themselves, through promoting knowledge, choice and control over their lives and decisions by:

- being reliable, honest and showing respect

- listening to service users, seeking and starting with their agendas

- providing independent, reliable and up-to-date information to support service users to think through options and reach decisions. This would include providing information and advice about income maintenance and other formal services and the resources for support and day-to-day living available from other organisations in the locality

- supporting people to think through what they want to do and how to achieve it

- supporting service users in their dealings and negotiations with other, sometimes hostile, state agencies and social institutions

- supporting service users to speak for themselves, as well as acting as advocates for them within and outside their organisation

- demonstrating the personal qualities highlighted by service users and their organisations and basing equal and open relationships with them on these

- working to enable service users to retain as much control over their lives as possible and over the choices that they make.

Blocks to be overcome

Social work practitioners and service users identified a number of obstacles to moving towards the kind of social work that they thought was needed. Their feeling was that good social work practice was often difficult to sustain in day-to-day work, although the relationship, the time and the process is actually what service users think is key to a good service. The sense was that these aspects of practice were often marginalised by their organisations and in the ways practice is managed. Examples given included:

- organisations that concentrate on structures and procedures rather than on service and practice that encourage independence, value and draw on the experience and knowledge of people using services

- practice that continues to fit people into services based on the model of safety-net and mass provision

- an 'expert' model where the social worker decides what should be done and operates on a user-friendly rather than a user-centred or user-controlled approach

- social workers, managers and policy makers who fear losing control when service users gain power and control over their lives; social services organisations, including general councils and national training organisations, set standards of practice and codes of conduct, and retain control through the regulation and inspection of services

- models of management which are concerned with command and control, when flexible, inclusive and responsive services require management that encourages innovation and decision making at the grassroots

- the belief that structures are all-important rather than the relationships that are built up at local level and with people using services

- the failure to recognise that people who use services understand rationing, are effective in allocating resources and have a key interest in being involved in decisions about resource allocation

- the absence of national user-led service and practice standards, so that the support people who use services get becomes a lottery, arbitrary and unequal.

(NISW 2001)

One hope for the future is that service user participation is now built in to the structure of new regulatory and standard-setting organisations and that there has been extensive consultation on the new codes of conduct and on the occupational standards for social work practice. These combined approaches should lead to a shared understanding between service users, practitioners, managers and government about what is required of social work and social care practitioners. This will need careful monitoring because the control mechanisms described above are still in place and may even be strengthened by the inspection mechanisms imposed by the Care Standards Act and its equivalents in other parts of the UK.

What needs to change

If practitioners are to play a more effective part and their knowledge is to influence the future development of social work, then much needs to change. Crucially this concerns the reassessment, repositioning and revaluing of social work practice and practitioners. It demands a new and equal role for social work practitioners. Practitioners and service users identify a wide range of key components for such change. These include the following.

The skills and expertise of social workers must be valued and used appropriately

Over the past thirty years, the time spent in direct work with service users and carers has decreased to about 20 per cent (Levin and Webb 1997). The main causes of this are increased administration and caseloads. Social workers can be carrying caseloads of 130 or more under some management systems. At this level the usual option is to concentrate on assessment of eligibility and then to move on. The supportive elements of social work are then lost as there is no time for them. As a result social work is increasingly devalued as a profession and the skills associated with it are being lost. Experienced social workers confirm the findings of the Social Services Inspectorate that all too often they had to 'smuggle' in their skills, almost as if they were ashamed of them (Platt 1998).

Social work practitioners should be more centrally involved in developing social work policies and practice

Social work practitioners are seldom involved in discussions about changes in the policies, services or structuring of their organisation, even though these often have a profound impact on their work and on the people they are working with. It is essential that social workers and service users are more fully and equally involved in the development of social work policy and practice in the future. As in health, a distinction needs to be drawn between the perspectives of practitioners and managers. Managers should not speak for practitioners who have the skills to communicate for themselves what they need to have in place to work as effectively as possible to work with service users.

Develop greater clarity about the role and expectations of social work

This is increasingly important as more and more work is carried out in multidisciplinary teams and organisations. The role of social work within the modernising agenda has not been properly thought through because it has been given a much lower priority than health or education. Yet if social work is to be effective its role in problem solving, negotiating working with conflict, securing people's rights and entitlements, and acting as a bridge between people and organisations has to be recognised by employers and employing organisations. Social work is a service in its own right. It is particularly significant in complex assessments, in tailoring, sustaining and renegotiating complex packages of support. Skills in working with distress, grief and loss, in mediating in relationships, are all to often under-used. Well used, these skills could avoid the inappropriate allocation of resources which do not promote the independence of service users and which undermine rather than underpin a person's social and support networks. At its best social work has the ability to:

- see people holistically as people and not as a set of deficits and problems
- understand and support the relationships and connections in their lives
- support people in working out what it is they want to do, often at very distressing and complicated times in their lives
- recognise and seek to challenge, rather than ignore, the constraints and discrimination which they experience in society

- support people to achieve what they want in their lives without denying their rights or infringing the rights of others.

Social work as integral to provision and not an add-on

Social workers are now increasingly employed in a range of organisations outside social care, in commercial and voluntary as well as statutory services. It is crucial that social work is recognised as an integral part of these services rather than just an add-on to them. An integrated approach requires recognition of the knowledge created through their practice. The means have to be found of making front line information an essential component of policy and service development. The complexity of the work has to be accepted and systems put in place to enable innovation and risks to be managed.

Making lifelong learning and continued professional development routine

Lifelong learning is recognised as part of everyone's personal life and essential to employment. In contrast to health policy and professions, the emphasis in social work on continuing professional development has been given less significance in the past. This has to change rapidly if social work is to fulfil its potential in promoting practice that is liberating for people who use services. As one practitioner said, 'Without continuing development, your practice can get stuck. There has to be progression through training'. Continuing professional development has to become the norm and part of work-based learning. That requires social workers at their desks to have routine direct access to research and to the knowledge created with and by people using services, practitioners and managers. This does not exist at the moment for many social work practitioners and hinders them in learning on and from the job. It prevents service users having access to the best available information when reaching decisions about their lives that are often difficult and life changing.

Social work is often a complex and demanding high-risk activity, yet the preparation time for qualification (even with the introduction of the new social work degree and qualification) is short in comparison with other professions requiring similar levels of skills, experience and sensitivity.

Post-qualifying and advanced training is no less important in social work than in these other professions. Promotion in social work is almost invariably out of practice, a further reflection of the low value placed on social work practice. New promotion routes within practice must be developed and consideration given to developing an equivalent of the new nurse consultant role. So far, where equivalents have been developed in social work they have tended to be based on managerial or advisory roles, again distancing people from practice. Expert practice is something that needs to be valued, because it is integral to delivering a good service and as such it deserves to be managed well and supported.

The acceptance of learning networks as part of practice development

There is often a difference of view between social work practitioners and their managers about the value of professional networks. Managers may see them as social events that offer little to the work of the organisation. In contrast, practitioners frequently see them as essential to changing practice. It is ironic that the development of networks is seen as important for people using services but less so for social workers. The workshop organised by and for social work practitioners on which this material is partly based was originally recommended by a group of service users who were astonished that there were so few opportunities for practitioners to network. Yet learning across organisations and professional groups, sharing common problems, approaches, information and resources, finding colleagues who can provide support to deal with stressful and very complex problems, is a recognised method of professional development in many fields. A well-organised network is an essential resource in specialist areas where there may be no one else working in the same field within their organisation. Without them, workers can be very isolated. There are well-organised networks in some areas of social work practice, for example palliative care and in social work with deaf communities, although there is a national shortage of qualified and experienced social workers to work effectively with deaf people. Both, however, are areas that are contributing to practice development. A social worker at the Social Work 2000 seminar said: 'An active and lively network helps support our practice especially when you are working in areas like palliative care, or working with deaf or blind people. You can be very isolated in the organisation'. These networks will become even more important as more and more social workers move into multidisciplinary teams and organisations. The issue of how social work develops cannot be addressed only through providing individual professional supervision to isolated workers. Opportunities for developing a collective analysis and voice will become vital.

Improving social work's image and developing an effective voice

The early 2000s have seen the danger of losing the critical mass of skilled practitioners. A better image of social work and social workers is essential both for good practice and the future of the profession. It would give practitioners the confidence and more possibilities to develop their practice and to promote its value. A better image is crucial to attracting the next generation into social work and to retaining those currently in the work, and could attract former social workers back.

The 2001 recruitment and retention campaign in each of the countries of the UK seems to have had some success. However, improving social work's image is far more than a public relations exercise. It will not be achieved without social work's strengths being both more evident and better communicated. Social work is most closely associated with child protection in the public mind and it has reinforced this image itself, even though it is a very small proportion of the work. Yet this is its most controversial and arguably least successful area. More effort needs to be given to highlighting areas of particular achievement, for example work with people with learning difficulties, in challenging discrimination and within specialist palliative care (Croft 1999). One of the tasks of educators and trainers, and managers of front-line practice is to enable social workers to articulate to the general public what they do.

At the beginning of the twenty-first century there is no effective voice for social work, no authoritative organisation or institution that speaks up for social work as there is, for example, for medicine or nursing. As one participant at the Social Work 2000 seminar put it, 'We are better at advocating for other people than for ourselves'. Another commented: 'Social work is a profession that is sometimes belittled by other professions. We should look at ourselves and the ability we have to work with people in an holistic way'. This is a major gap that needs to be filled to change the image of social work, to improve the reality and to counter the negative and inaccurate stereotypes of social work and social workers. A powerful voice is essential for social work to play its full part in supporting user-controlled and user-centred provision, equal partnerships across organisations, professions and sectors, and in order to tailor services practice and services to better support individuals, families and communities.

Including the experience and knowledge of practitioners

The increasing political emphasis on 'evidence-based' policy in health and social care has highlighted the need to re-examine the knowledge base of social work and social care. So far two key sources of knowledge have tended to be neglected in the their construction. These are the knowledge and experience of service users and that of practitioners. SCIE, the Social Care Institute for Excellence – the social care equivalent of health's NICE (the National Institute for Clinical Excellence) – has now been established to develop the knowledge base of social care. In its early days, all the signs are that it is committed to an inclusive approach to knowledge formation which includes the knowledge of practitioners. This provides an important opportunity as well as the impetus for social work practitioners' knowledge to influence policy and practice. More work will need to be done to identify effective ways to do this and ensure that practitioners' grass-roots knowledge is both fully accessed and influential in the development of policy and practice. This process is likely to include encouraging practitioner research and evaluations by practitioners and developing participatory ways of including practitioners' views and experience and ensuring they are included in processes of review, audit and inspection.

Developing a fully inclusive workforce

While social work as an institution has highlighted issues of discrimination and developed the concept of 'anti-oppressive practice', it has frequently failed to ensure equal opportunities within its workforce, particularly around issues of disability. Social work and social care do not have a strong track record in recruiting suitably qualified workers with experience of using services. This has tended to reinforce rather than challenge the 'them and us' of social work. There is no reason why suitably qualified disabled people, mental health service users, people living with HIV/AIDS, people with learning difficulties and with experience as 'looked after' children could not be recruited in larger numbers to the social work workforce. More often than not, having an impairment or experience of using mental health services has been seen as a negative and something the worker needs to conceal if possible. As was said at the Social Work 2000 seminar:

> It took me 18 months to get my first job after qualifying. There is a huge problem about disability. We don't start on the same rung of the ladder … the profession is not very caring. It is uneasy being with blind people. They want to help but don't know how. (Social worker with a visual impairment)

> Managers don't understand the needs of deaf social workers or service users when there are cultural and language issues relating to British Sign Language (BSL). (Deaf social worker)

Service user workers highlight the frequent failure of their organisations and managers to be supportive of their difference and this means that their practice may have to develop in spite of and not because of the way it is managed. Similarly workers who experience distress or acquire impairments frequently describe the failure of their organisations to respond positively and supportively. This needs to change. Direct experience of social care services should be seen as a valued plus and built into job and person specifications. Service users' concerns about 'glass ceilings' and their ghettoisation should also be challenged (Gell 2001). At a major national mental health service user–worker conference in 2001, problems of discrimination in health and social care employment practice were repeatedly highlighted. The Disability Discrimination Act, now extended to cover education, backed up the Disability Rights Commission offers the prospect of making a real difference here. User-controlled services are also offering examples of good practice in employing and promoting service users, although their frequently limited and insecure funding makes it difficult for them to offer an adequate career structure.

Increasing the involvement of practitioners in social work education and training

So far, the involvement of current practitioners in social work education has mainly been confined to roles as placement supervisors and practice teachers. While this connection with the 'field' is undoubtedly important and offers some grounding (which has become increasing difficult to ensure) in practical realities, it also highlights and reinforces the potential gulf between 'school' and practice agency. Although the requirements for the new social work qualification requires the involvement of service users, the implementation starts from this very low base. In addition, although the emphasis is on social work being closely connected with the practical and day-to-day realities of service users' lives, there is little encouragement for educators on professional education and training courses to maintain practice. It is rare for heads of department or senior staff to have current or recent practice experience. Joint appointments have shown the benefits of maintaining such links, but now these are more likely to result from the 'casualisation' of education and training with staff retained on part-time temporary contracts that create additional problems of stress, insecurity and turnover. Current and recent practice experience should be identified as desirable when recruiting staff and new schemes developed to foster and extend joint appointments and opportunities for teaching staff to maintain practice in mainstream social work.

Conclusion

A massive and coherent agenda for the future of social work emerges from practitioners – when they are offered opportunities to develop their views. It poses the existing institutions with an enormous challenge. The gap between what social workers experience and their aspirations is a measure of how long they and their views and proposals have been ignored or excluded. For at least twenty years social work and social care have been dominated by a managerialism which has devalued the experience and knowledge of both service users and practitioners.

Concern has continued that social work and social services are used to implement managerialist and authoritarian welfare policies and that social work education is under tightening bureaucratic control (Payne 1994; Jones 1998). Commentators fear that social work has itself internalised the market-led political ideologies that are associated with the increasing poverty, social injustice and division which it is meant to counter, or been by-passed by them (Holman 1993; Jordan and Jordan 2000). At the same time, social work is seen as under constant attack from the media and political right (for example, Marsland 1993; also see *Community Care* Speak Out campaign during 2000).

In 2001, the annual Community Care Live event brought together service users and practitioners involved in the Social Work 2000 seminar and the SUET workshop on user involvement in training to debate the future of social care practice. As one panel member, Gloria Gifford, said:

> The power imbalance that exists between social workers and users is made worse by the lack of clarity about what social workers do – the lack of public knowledge of what you do. It is confusing for service users who don't know what you do, whether you do it well, whether you are to be trusted. Are you someone on our side, who can advocate on our behalf, or are you non-uniformed police? Are you there to support us, or to disarm us? The challenge for service users and social workers is surely to work together – to develop a relationship that is empowering for both parties.

Although participants did not minimise the problems, there was also a sense of optimism for the future. There was recognition that service users frequently valued practitioners and were supportive of their efforts, even if they often experienced their agencies as oppressive and unhelpful. While service users often felt marginalised in social work and social care there was a sense in which they saw practitioners as even more marginalised. People saw the way forward as developing shared understanding, links and collaboration between service users and practitioners. The disabled people's movement has developed the slogan 'Nothing About Us Without Us' to highlight its demands. As participants at this session said, it is now time for social work practitioners to adopt the same slogan to secure their inclusion the future development of social work policy, practice and research. Extending this principle to the involvement of practitioners and service users in the management and monitoring of practice and social services organisations should result in more sensitive and effective services.

References

Beresford, P. (2002) 'Thinking about 'Mental Health': Towards a social model.' *Journal of Mental Health 6*, 11, 581–584.

Beresford, P. and Trevillion, S. (1995) *Developing Skills for Community Care: A Collaborative Approach.* Aldershot: Arena.

Croft, S. (1999) 'How Can I Leave Them?: Towards an empowering social work practice with women who are dying.' In B. Fawcett, M. Galloway and J. Perrins (eds) *Feminism and Social Work in the Year 2000: Conflicts and Controversies.* Bradford: Department of Applied Social Studies, University of Bradford.

Department of Health (2002) *Howard Shipman's Clinical Practice 1974–1998: A Clinical Audit Commissioned by the Chief Medical Officer of Health.* London: Department of Health.

Gell, C. (ed) (2001) *Valuing Experience.* London: Institute for Applied Health and Social Policy, King's College.

Harding, T. and Beresford, P. (eds) (1996) *The Services We Expect: What Service Users and Carers Want From Social Services Workers.* London: National Institute for Social Work.

Holman, B. (1993) *A New Deal for Social Welfare.* Oxford: Lion Publishing.

Home Office (2001) *Race Relations (Amendment) Act 2000: New Laws for a Successful Multi-Racial Britain.* London: HMSO.

Jones, C. (1998) 'Social Work And Society.' In R. Adams, L. Dominelli and M. Payne (eds) *Social Work: Themes, Issues and Critical Debates.* Basingstoke: Macmillan, 34–43.

Jordan, B. and Jordan, C. (2000) *Social Work and the Third Way.* London: Sage.

Kennedy, I. (2001) *Inquiry into Children's Heart Surgery at the Bristol Infirmary.* London: Department of Health.

Levin, E. and Webb, S. (1997) *Social Work and Community Care: Changing Roles and Tasks.* London: National Institute for Social Work.

Marsland, D. (1993) 'Social Workers, The Final Folly of The Sixties.' *Daily Mail,* 21 June, 8.

NISW (National Institute for Social Work) (1999) *National Debate on the Future of Social Work: Creating a new agenda.* London: National Institute for Social Work.

NISW (National Institute for Social Work) (2000) *Modernising Social Work: Social work in the Modernising Agenda.* London: National Institute for Social Work.

NISW (National Institute for Social Work) (2001) *Putting the Person First: Service Users' Views on the Introduction of Codes of Conduct and Practice for Social Care Workers by the Four National Care Councils.* London: National Institute for Social Work.

Oliver, M. (1983) *Social Work with Disabled People.* London: Macmillan.

Payne, M. (1994) 'The End of British Social Work.' *Professional Social Work*, 5 February.

Platt, D. (1998) 'The Changing Role of Social Work.' Paper presented at the conference, National Debate On The Future Of Social Work, London, 23 September.

TOPSS (Training Organisation for the Personal Social Services) (2002) *National Occupational Standards for Social Work.* www.topss.org.uk

CHAPTER 3

Users Influencing the Management of Practice

Michael Turner and Clare Evans

The vision and leadership of service users working at both a national and local level is having a major influence on empowerment practice. The expertise users bring requires a redefinition of the professional role and the support that workers need in order to carry out that role. Where users have had a real input in this process it is possible to see the implications for the management of practice. The opportunities for service users to take on leadership roles are theoretically present throughout the social care system. If they are to be achieved there needs to be present a strong organisation controlled by users alongside the social care provider organisation and changes to the culture of organisations providing social care.

Users' influence in national policy making has direct implications for the management of front line staff. The most recent example of this affecting disabled people as users and all social services departments has been the Community Care (Direct Payments) Act of 1996. This legislation was the direct result of many years of campaigning for the right to control over their support by the disabled people's independent living movement. Prior to 1996, as well as sustained lobbying for change by disabled people at a national level, disability organisations were working with local authorities in many areas to establish schemes to bypass laws which restricted councils from making payments to individuals and thus prevented social services departments from making direct payments in lieu of services. In many areas so-called 'third-party schemes' were set up that allowed the local authority to make a grant to an independent body which was then able to make payments to disabled people.

Most of these schemes were set up and run by organisations that were controlled by disabled people who then developed the expertise and detailed knowledge to provide advice on employment and other issues required by people employing their own personal assistants. When the Act was passed in 1996 that enabled local authorities to make direct payments themselves, the expertise and experience to make the system work lay with disabled people rather than social services employees. During the passage of the legislation disabled people had been on a working group advising the Department of Health and the minister responsible for the new law, and officials also made fact-finding visits to many of the third-party schemes that were showing how direct payments could work in practice. The government guidance that accompanied the new law recommended that local authorities should establish support services for direct payments users and that such services should be based in disabled people's organisations. It also explicitly recognised the expertise of disabled people in this area by funding the establishment of the National Centre for Independent Living, an offshoot of the British Council of Disabled People, which enables local authorities to access the advice of disabled consultants on the establishment of direct payments schemes.

This change in social policy gives a strong example of how the influence of service users, in this case, disabled people, can have an impact, and the implications this has for redefining the professional role of staff and its management. Each local authority – even those that had third-party schemes prior to the legislation – has had to struggle with which parts of the care management and planning process remain in-house and which are best provided externally, usually through the auspices of a centre for independent living or another organisation run by disabled people. Professionals have had to recognise the value of expertise within disabled people's organisations in order to provide the best service to direct payments users. However, this does mean that professionals have no role in the new system. Care managers remain responsible for the assessment of need upon which direct payments are based – although disabled people are still pressing for greater emphasis on self-assessment – and can be crucial to whether or not a disabled person is able to access direct payments. Bewley's (2000) assessment of progress for people with learning difficulties in obtaining direct payments goes as far as to suggest that every person with a learning difficulty who has been successful in accessing direct payments has had someone to champion their cause and that, on occasion, this has been their care manager. Bewley argues that such care managers are the exception to the rule and people with learning difficulties often have to battle with teams and departments that are very reluctant to support direct payments.

A user-controlled demonstration project that carried out a Best Value Review of Direct Payments in Wiltshire (Evans and Carmichael 2002) found that one of the blocks to implementation was that care managers lacked knowledge and information for users about the direct payments option.

If such practice does not bode well for service users it has even stronger implications for the practitioners themselves. The legislation for direct payments passed by a Conservative government has been supported enthusiastically by the Labour administration elected in 1997. Restrictions on eligibility for direct payments were removed in 1999 making them available to people over 65 years old and has encouraged their take-up by a wider group of service users, including people with learning difficulties, disabled young people and their parents. The challenge for social services departments in the light of this commitment from central government is to set targets to increase take-up of direct payments. The key to achieving these targets will be whether care managers have the skills to support and encourage disabled people's moves towards independence rather than acting as barriers and impeding their progress. The negative approach encountered by Bewley suggests that this change has not yet been embraced by many care managers or their superiors, and that this failure means that they are missing out on a 'fantastic opportunity for care managers to be inspired by their job' (p.15). A further issue developing as direct payments become mainstream is that the information and advice services contracted by social services are increasingly being provided by organisations other than the local organisation of disabled people building on their experiences as service users and peer support. Mainstreaming innovations like direct payments often carry with it the risk that vital elements are omitted and this process undermines the benefits to the service user. Direct payments are based on the philosophy of independent living. The challenge for managers then is how the ethos of independent living associated with direct payments in the disabled people's movement is maintained.

There is a wider issue of quality of care management and its implications for managers of front line staff. Recognising users' right to be involved in, and indeed leading, the community care assessment process requires care managers to play an enabling role rather than that of being the 'professional who knows best'. Time restraints and the need for care managers to act as gatekeepers of limited resources conspire to work against this redefined role so that empowering care management practice often seems to be delivered despite the system rather than because of it. Parsloe and Stevenson (1993) have written of the need to have empowered workers if service users themselves are to be empowered. They found a considerable amount of good practice on this front but suggested that this was far from the norm in most services. They describe the manager's role in relation to this situation as being to enable the practitioner to recognise tensions such as those between budgets and the needs of users and between users and carers, and to hold fast to the vision and the goal of empowerment. For practitioners to achieve this they need the space to address ethical and professional issues as well as managerial and budgetary matters.

Managers of social care workers such as home care workers also need to help staff to understand the tensions in their jobs between enabling the service user and respecting their views and choices, and maintaining agency systems in relation to time keeping, health and safety policies, etc. Cunningham (2000) has demonstrated the oppressive effects on service users of local authorities' stringent interpretation of European legislation on moving and handling in order to protect themselves from possible litigation from staff who are injured at work. Cunningham found the interpretation of the laws and subsequent training of staff without sufficient involvement of service users has severely restricted the lives of many service users by requiring them to be dependent on the use of hoists and extra staff. The service users who took part in Cunningham's study believed it was a task for professionals to ensure, with input from service users, that staff have suitable training in lifting and handling techniques and that appropriate equipment should be available.

Disabled people have learnt a range of strategies to demonstrate their leadership abilities and the role that they can play in social policy by both challenging the system itself and influencing the planning of services and the training of staff. European legislation on human rights and the Disability Discrimination Act will further enable service users to challenge disempowerment and discrimination and will establish case law relating to discriminatory practice. This legislation, combined with social policy, creates the potential for a changed relationship with professionals and their organisations. In health as well as social care the trend is for service users to become active contributors to constructing their own lives, the outcomes of service provision and practice.

One growing area of users' influence is that of user workers. In addition to social care staff who identify themselves as service users a further 25 per cent of social care staff are family carers (Balloch *et al.*1999). Consultations with service users have often found that they believe social care agencies would increase their credibility considerably if they employed more service users. However, evidence suggests (Rooke-Matthews and Lindow 1998) that the direct experience of being or having been a service user is not valued by social care agencies and that disclosing use of mental health services leads to almost certain rejection in the recruitment process. During our experience in Wiltshire, one family carer spoke of it not being acceptable to talk about his anorexic daughter in his role as a manager, and a planning officer referred to being unable to speak of the difficulties she had with attending evening meetings because of her role providing support for her partner who was disabled. The same appears to be true of people with physical impairments, with one writer (Lewis 2000) lamenting, 'Why is it then that the only experience most of us may have of a disabled professional in these areas is of the disabled Dr Kerry Weaver in the American TV series *ER*?' The support required by service users in order to work is not always available from employers in the social care sector and most front-line managers are unaware of the support available to disabled people in jobs through the Employment Service's Access to Work scheme that will meet the costs of specialist equipment and support workers. It is more common for managers to make assumptions about disabled people and other service users' inability to do a given job than to investigate such options.

The Disability Discrimination Act is enabling more disabled people to challenge the most obvious instances of discrimination in relation to employment, but discrimination is actually enshrined in the new legislation that will dictate who can and cannot work in social care. The Care Standards Act of 2000 contains a clause that anyone registering with the new social care councils must be 'physically and mentally fit to do the job', which both the British Association of Social Workers and the Disability Rights Commission have condemned as discriminatory (Lewis 2000). There remains a considerable amount of prejudice to be challenged at all levels before service users begin to play a full role in service provision.

In order for service users to provide the vision and leadership to shape how social care agencies develop and become user led, a shift in culture is needed to change attitudes to be receptive to a user-led approach. Involving users in the training of staff in a number of ways is an effective means of changing that culture and of enabling staff that gain the skills to work in a way that is empowering to service users. The role disabled people can play in training managers on the principles of disability equality and user involvement has been demonstrated by Morris and Hemmings (1997). Their project looked at training for disabled people in their rights as service users and at disabled people providing training to social services departments on issues such as user involvement, and led to the establishment of a network of user-trainers.

Evans and Hughes (1993) reported on the experience of service users in Wiltshire participating in care management training during the introduction of community care in the 1990s which led to a significant change in culture across the whole social services department for the county. The user-controlled organisation in Wiltshire also has experience of providing supervision for students on the Diploma in Social Work and has shown that this has a unique effect on their subsequent practice once they are qualified. Students placed at the offices of the Wiltshire and Swindon Users' Network were people who previously had felt that they had advanced ideas on user involvement and empowering work practice. Nevertheless they found working within an entirely user-controlled organisation, where professional status carried no weight and they were judged simply on how effective they were in empowering users, was a significant and important learning experience. Evaluation of this work by the University of Bristol found that students on these placements experienced an initial loss of confidence, and it was important for the user providing supervision for the student to recognise and be sensitive to the situation of the student. It is not only students who lose confidence during change. The managers of front line workers equally need support to move towards frameworks and standards that focus practice on outcomes that are defined by service users.

Users' vision and leadership needs to influence all tiers of an organisation if it is to achieve the change in culture to empowering practice. 'Riddling the system' was the phrase adopted by service users in Wiltshire to describe the strategy of involving users in all aspects of the county's social service department's work towards this goal. Senior managers had an important role as active allies in encouraging all staff to embrace this way of working in Wiltshire, as they would elsewhere. The support of elected members of the council was also crucial, with the relationships in Wiltshire being developed through regular meetings between elected members of the council's social services committee and service user representatives who had themselves been elected.

The management of practice needs to reflect on its effectiveness and enable staff to have confidence in encouraging feedback from users. There has been much emphasis in recent years on developing effective complaints procedures within social care agencies. It is important that all individual users have the right to complain and that complaints policies are widely publicised in order for users to be aware of this right and how it can be exercised, and to feel safe from recrimination or loss of service. However, taking issues raised in complaints seriously is only a small part of receiving feedback on effective practice from service users.

To maintain the quality of services it is necessary to build in ongoing systems to get regular feedback from users. In the year 2000 the President of the Association of Directors of Social Services, Jo Williams, said:

> I am convinced that we must move away from traditional surveyswhich look at whether users and carers are satisfied with our servicestowards an approach which considers more carefully what service users and carers value. The approach needs to be not checking but learning. (Presedential speech, Annual Social Services Conference 2000)

Entering into a dialogue with users thorough regular meetings that are facilitated by independent user groups attached to services provides an opportunity for both users and practitioners to develop their skills and gain confidence. The Leonard Cheshire Disabled People's Forum was set up to achieve exactly this and has quarterly meetings in each of its ten regions to collect feedback from users about its services and to engage with senior managers about changing any services that are found to be less than satisfactory. For practitioners the regular feedback acts as a reminder of the need to work in a user-centred way at all times (Disabled People's Forum 2000).

The growing stress on practitioners identifying outcomes of their work with individual service users has the potential for profound impact on the management of front line staff. The move towards measuring outcomes as opposed to evaluation in terms of process has been well document by Qureshi and Nocoon (1996). The impact of the emphasis on outcomes on practice has become fully evident through the work on user perspectives on outcomes carried out by the Shaping Our Lives project. This has demonstrated the complexity of outcome definitions. This user-controlled project grew out of work around standards in social care carried out by Harding and Beresford (1996). The starting-point for the project was the rejection of the imposition of professionally defined outcomes as measures and focused on the need for each individual service user to be able to define their own outcomes in relation to their perceived needs. This starting-point and the work of the project showed that simply involving users in outcomes at the point of measurement was a fruitless activity: if users are to have a say at this point they must first have a say in the setting of the outcomes. The project also found that, in defining the outcomes they wanted to achieve, users took into account their whole lives rather than the narrowly defined concepts of individual need used in social care. Users described the need for a more holistic approach to services and support. *Putting the Person First* (NISW 2000), a leaflet produced by the project, states that services should 'address the whole range of people's needs, recognising that these needs are interconnected and cannot be separated out to fit conveniently with the current structures of service provision'.

Similar points have been made by other initiatives. The user-controlled Strategies for Living project has demonstrated how alternative therapies, spiritualism and social networks can enable mental health service users/survivors to address their distress more effectively than traditional services. The government-sponsored Better Government for Older People initiative has worked to develop the dialogue between older people and local authorities and health services in 28 pilot areas. As well as addressing issues around services specifically aimed at older people, the programme highlighted that a wide range of public services have an impact on their quality of life, such as house design, public transport and neighbourhood safety. Similar diversity came out in work carried out by older people in Wiltshire some years earlier in a project that started with the aim of involving older people in planning and developing social services and went on to address a much wider range of issues (Wiltshire and Swindon Users' Network 1997).

The implications of this holistic approach for front line staff and for social care establishment are wide ranging, indicating not only that it is not appropriate to use predefined outcomes but that significant change is needed in the services provided. The key issues seem to centre around choice and control, with Shaping Our Lives noting that while many users of traditional services struggled to identify the outcomes they achieved from the support that they received, people who used direct payment could clearly identify the outcomes in terms of independence and having control of their lives. Exactly how – and whether – such changes impact on front line services remains to be seen, though Shaping Our Lives clearly advocates constructive collaboration and an evolutionary approach to change.

Another key issue for practice identified by the work of Shaping Our Lives was that process and outcome are not separated when viewed from the users' perspectives. This view – which goes contrary to previous thinking on outcomes – indicates that how a user feels at the end of a task being carried out is affected by the attitudes of the staff who deliver the service as well as the satisfactory completion of the task, for example, for someone who needs assistance getting up and getting dressed in the morning, a simple measure of being dressed and ready to start the day does not adequately describe the outcome experienced by the service user. For the user, feeling that they have had choice and control over the process and that the assistance has been provided in a friendly and supportive manner affects how they feel at the outcome and the importance of those feelings should not be underestimated. Being dressed may be a recordable outcome, but if you have had to fight to wear what you want to wear, or even just had unfriendly silence through the process, the outcome does not include a positive frame of mind – particularly when you face the same process day in, day out. The clear implication for managing front line practice is that, while outcomes are rightly being given greater weight, practitioners should not lose sight of the importance of good process. Shaping Our Lives makes the point concisely, saying that there can be no good outcomes without good processes of service delivery.

The current emphasis on measuring the quality of service rather than the earlier emphasis on resource input is welcomed by users since outcomes measure the difference that a service makes to their lives on an everyday basis. However, as the Shaping Our Lives project has shown, unless users are involved in defining quality measures such an emphasis can focus on the wrong priority areas and inappropriate measures can be used. The development of user-defined monitoring systems provides a formal approach to ongoing measurement of standards of quality. Such work has already been carried out the Sainsbury Centre for Mental Health with its user-focused monitoring project (Rose 1999). This has identified the need for professionals to recognise two roles for service users –those of informants and of evaluators. The benefits of involving users in this way were identified as 'improved information about what matters to users, better targeted services based on identified needs and better working relationships between staff, users and carers'. The Shaping Our Lives project has also moved on to practical work and in 2000 began work with four local user groups on development projects on user-controlled monitoring of outcomes with the aim of developing models of good practice. Such models offer practitioners the opportunity of learning how similar monitoring work can be done within their own agencies.

Knowledge-based practice formalises the model of practitioners continuously reflecting on and addressing the effectiveness of their work through feedback. Many issues are raised by professional advocates for this practice. For example, what counts as evidence and how is it measured? In some academic situations users have become passive victims in the professional debate about qualitative and quantitative methods. Meanwhile, practitioners are slow to develop ongoing processes to evaluate their work from users' perspectives. They need the opportunity to gain skills to collect users' views – ideally working with users to identify priorities and give advice about the best ways of collecting users' views. Local government's corporate Best Value policies of reviewing services will need to recognise the particular knowledge and skills needed to contact 'hard-to-reach' service users. The project carrying out a user-controlled Best Value Review of Direct Payments (Evans and Carmichael 2002) demonstrates the gains of such user influence.

The new millennium has started with a plethora of national standard-setting initiatives from central government. Once adopted such standards will enable practitioners to measure their own practice and provide the means for users to challenge service delivery that falls below standard. The opportunity for users to be involved in influencing these standards as they are constructed is essential to ensuring their relevance to the realities experienced by service users. Both good and bad practice have been demonstrated in research carried out with users by the Shaping Our Lives project as part of the development of the codes of conduct and practice for the General Social Care Council (NISW 2001). This report picked up on many issues around the quality of practice made by Harding and Beresford (1996), and found little indication that any great progress had been made. Key issues around quality identified by users who contributed to the study included respecting the user, good time keeping, being accessible, keeping confidentiality and respecting privacy, treating all users equally, and supporting users to keep control over their lives rather than taking it away. Many of those questioned had had experienced failure in relation to these issues and these findings confirm those of Shaping Our Lives on the inherent link between outcome and process, and therefore on front line practice as crucial to quality outcomes for service users. One of its most interesting and challenging implications for practice was the importance of the human qualities of the social care workers. The phrase 'putting the person first' was repeatedly used to describe what users meant by the best-quality practice, and they considered this a key aspect of good practice. From the evidence of these studies, users clearly want the idea of putting the person first to become a guiding principle for practice in social care, but after more than a decade of supposedly 'needs-led' services, they are all too aware of the political and resource issues that come between such ideas and reality.

The policy context in which front line practitioners work is constantly changing and so social workers need management support in adapting to new ways of working to reflect these changes. Direct payments were developed within the broader context of disabled people influencing the more general planning of services and challenging purchasers to adopt the social model of disability as a basis for service planning (Priestly 1999). The implications of the social model of disability and concepts of independent living developed from it have influenced the provision of services for disabled people away from day centres and residential care to individual support in the community with an emphasis on removing the barriers to more integrated life in the community based on choice and control. The constraints on social service practitioners and their organisations' ability to change barriers to accessible transport and employment opportunities illustrate the limitations on the social care sector in supporting independent living for disabled people directly. This does not mean that they are powerless. They can enable services users to gain confidence to participate through funding service-user organisations, they can support service users to empower themselves to campaign for changes in these barriers directly, and they can acknowledge through their planning, practice and management that transport, employment and housing are essential components of independent living.

During the 1990s the community care planning structures developed in different ways. In some local authorities it was led by social work practitioners whereas in others users had the opportunity of playing a part in the design of the new structures. Here it was possible to build bottom-up structures where local user groups set the agenda to inform local interagency planning groups which in turn set the agenda for the detail of strategic plans.

If users are to play a strong role in planning structures and in evaluating services they need to build strong user-controlled organisations. These provide a 'safe place' for users to develop the skills and confidence to participate effectively. Such strong organisations need long-term community development which requires senior managers to have confidence and be prepared to give space and resources to such initiatives. As well as empowering the user members to be involved these organisations are also able to act as user-controlled development agencies. The credibility of independent user workers facilitating groups of users and a commitment to reach out to marginalised users in turn gives statutory sector managers an enhanced quality of users' views to inform practice (Wiltshire and Swindon Users' Network 1997).

Regrettably, the evidence is that in many areas the development of user-controlled organisations is being hampered by lack of resources. A survey of services led by disabled people by Barnes, Mercer and Morgan (2000) noted both that the development of centres for independent living in Britain has been slow compared with other countries and that funding was a continuing problem for all the organisations that took part in the survey. Most organisations had less than two years of secured funding. While the issue about how much resources are available is a key one – and is in itself a political decision – Barnes, Mercer and Morgan also found that user-controlled organisations have substantial dilemmas about the types of services they want to provide and the requirements of funding bodies. This may have particular implications in relation to work around involvement, which in many areas seems to remain an optional extra rather than a key part of social care practice and provision.

Assessing the situation at the start of the new millennium is not easy. With so many conflicting messages and many initiatives set up by the Labour Government, elected in 1997, in their early stages, it is impossible to determine whether the outlook is positive or not.

Partnership working means social work practitioners now need to work across agencies and sometimes as a minority in the workplace alongside health service colleagues. Managers – sometimes working from a geographical distance – need to give practitioners professional competence and confidence to work from perspectives based on the social model of disability despite differing perspectives from other colleagues in other agencies. The establishment of primary care trusts has signalled the start of closer working between health care and social care staff and services, a move which would seem to reflect users' calls for a more holistic approach to support. However, it is also a move which has been accompanied by the suggestion that health services might take a lead in this joint approach, and the idea has even been broached that social services might become a part of the health service. This is an idea that causes some concern among service users, as anecdotal experience suggests that whatever the limitations of user involvement in social care, health care services are even further behind. This is not to say joint working is without promise, as long as service users are the central focus of the work. Where this is achieved the results can be positive, as in one example where the involvement of other users in training care managers from health and social services jointly demonstrated that their presence made practitioners drop their interagency rivalry and focus on the perspective of users (Evans and Hughes 1993).

Likewise, the new regulatory bodies for social care – the General Social Care Councils, the Care Standards Commission and TOPSS (Training Organisation for the Personal Social Services) – all have enormous potential if they can develop a focus on the perspective of users. In order to influence practice they must also be seen very clearly by practitioners, service users and the wider public as being focused on service users. The present Government does seem to be keen to promote a perspective of quality that is based on the views of service users and the 'carers' of service users. The Under Secretary of State for Health, John Hutton, told a conference organised by the *Guardian* and the National Institute for Social Work in 2000:

> I want us to think about how quality can be defined… A good place to begin is with users' and carers' experiences of social services. Their knowledge is key to what constitutes good services. I want us to listen and then apply the lessons learned from them… Users' views area crucial way of testing and assessing for quality in services.

However, what is less clear – and consequently very discouraging – is whether the drive for quality will be matched by resources. Quality cannot be divorced from adequate resources. One of the areas studied by Turner (2002) revealed a clear divide between the quality of service provided by staff employed directly by social services and those employed by agencies providing contracted services. The users reported that efforts to improve the quality of service from agency staff had been unsuccessful as a result of lack of enforcement, but there must also be a question of how far it is possible to maintain and improve standards in the face of pressure to reduce costs. In addition to providing resources for the services themselves, there is also an issue of funding service-user organisations so that there is an independent and user-controlled route for monitoring and evaluation of quality. The large numbers of service users receiving most of their services from the independent sector require new initiatives on user involvement to influence these services. The Disabled People's Forum developed by disabled development workers within Leonard Cheshire to empower their service users to participate effectively to influence practice, provides a model for other large independent social care providers (Disabled People's Form 1998, 1999, 2000).

Ensuring adequacy of resources is obviously outside the control of most managers, but there is also an issue around the use of available resources and ensuring that they are used to provide the services that people want and require rather than those deemed appropriate. Direct payments are perhaps the ultimate example of users controlling the way in which resources are used. At the time of writing only a small proportion of service users have access to direct payments, but the challenge for front-line managers at the start of the twenty-first century is to look at how this kind of control over services can be given to a greater number of users – through both direct payments and traditional services – so that they become truly empowered and have influence in the fullest sense of the word over the practice relating to their services.

References

Balloch, S., McLean, J. and Fisher, M. (1999) *Social Services: Working Under Pressure.* Bristol: Policy Press.

Barnes, C., Mercer, G. and Morgan, H. (2000) *Creating Independent Futures: An Evaluation of Services Led by Disabled People.* Leeds: The Disability Press.

Better Government for Older People/University of Warwick (2000) *Making a Difference – the Better Government for Older People Evaluation Summary.* Warwick: University of Warwick.

Bewley, C. (2000) 'Care Managers Can be Champions for Direct Payments.' *Care Plan* 6, 4, 13–16.

Cunningham, S. (2000) *Disability, Oppression and Public Policy.* Keighley: Independent Living Ltd.

Disabled People's Forum (1998) *Bottom Up Change.* London: Leonard Cheshire Foundation.

Disabled People's Forum (1999) *Riddling the System*. London: Leonard Cheshire
   Foundation.

Disabled People's Forum (2000) *Building On*. London: Leonard Cheshire Foundation.

Evans, C. (1997) *From Bobble Hats to Red Jackets*. Devizes, Wits: Wiltshire & Swindon
   Users' Network.

Evans, C. and Carmichael, A. (2002) *Users' Best Value: A Guide to User Involvement in
   Good Practice Reviews*. York: Joseph Rowntree Foundation.

Evans, C. and Hughes, M. (eds) (1993) *Tall Oaks From Little Acorns: The Wiltshire
   Experience of Involving Users in Training Professionals in Care Management*. Cherhill,
   Wilts: Wiltshire Community Care User Involvement Network.

Harding, T. and Beresford, P. (1996) *The Standards We Expect*. London: National
   Institute for Social Work.

Lewis, N. (2000) 'Social Work and the NHS – Where are the Disabled
   Professionals?' *Community Care*, 7–13 September.

NISW (National Institute for Social Work) (2001) *Putting the Person First: Service Users'
   Views on the Introduction of Codes of Conduct and Practice for Social Care Workers by
   the Four National Care Councils*. London: National Institute for Social Work.

Parsloe, P. and Stevenson, O. (1993) 'A Powerhouse for Change.' *Community Care*, 18
   February, 24–25.

Priestley, M. (1999) *Disability Politics and Community Care*. London: Jessica Kingsley
   Publishers.

Qureshi, H. and Nocon, A. (1996) *Outcomes of Community Care for Users and Carers*.
   Buckingham: Open University Press.

Rooke-Matthews, S. and Lindow, V. (1998) *A Survivors' Guide to Working In Mental
   Health Services*. London: Mind.

Rose, D. (1999) 'Do it Yourselves.' In *Mental Health Care 2*, 5, 174–7.

Turner, M. (2002) *Shaping Our Lives – From Outset to Outcome: What People Think of the
   Social Care they Use*. York: Joseph Rowntree Foundation.

Wiltshire and Swindon Users' Network (1997) *A Guide to Involving Older People and
   their Carers in the Planning of Local Health and Social Care Services: The Trowbridge
   Experience*. Wiltshire and Swindon Users' Network.

CHAPTER 4

Managing Practice in Black and Minority Ethnic Organisations

Yoni Ejo

A growing number of organisations has been set up and managed by and for people from black and minority ethnic communities because of considerable dissatisfaction with the lack of appropriate practice and the disproportionate level of control, as opposed to support, services directed towards these communities. This chapter uses the research on one of these, the Bibini Centre in Manchester. Set up in 1991, young people were and are involved in all aspects of its work, which includes residential and day care provision. Bibini now has over ten years experience of providing specialist services for young people from black and minority ethnic groups and a number of issues that were key in the management of practice are often not considered in the literature on managing practice: the organisation's origins, values and philosophy; its local, regional and national context; establishing culturally competent services where mainstream provision has failed; being a black-run voluntary organisation; responding to externally set standards in ways that hold to Bibini's mission. Active management of all of these provided the space in which culturally competent practice and services could flourish.

The Origins of the Bibini Centre

The Bibini Centre for Young People developed a range of services as a result of black communities' concern that they were not receiving equal access to services and support. Black managers have a great deal to contend with in most organisations, but there are specific issues which arise for a manager within a black agency. Here it is not only the individual members of staff and the people who use services that face discrimination in its many forms but also the organisation as a whole. Black organisations have to work in a context where there is a lack of culturally competent services and practice. These are key elements that shape the management role in specific ways.

A demographic context to our community-based work

The disadvantages which black children and families experience, especially when in social need, impact on many areas of black people's lives, especially in housing, health, social care services and economically. The 1991 census indicated that ethnic minority groups continued to be in a worse situation compared to Whites in terms of housing quality, overcrowding, concentration in disadvantaged areas and experience of high levels of segregation (Karn 1997; Peach 1996). These create stress within families and on children and young people. In addition Manchester is disproportionately affected by economic deprivation and poverty, and has a high proportion of unemployed residents. Seventeen per cent are unemployed and more than 33 per cent of the population are dependent on income support. The city has the highest proportion of housing benefit recipients in the UK – 46 per cent of households (Manchester Management Action Plan 2001). Many of the families the Bibini Centre works with are subjected to extreme economic deprivation and may have additional difficulties in securing support and access to services. The impact of racism and discrimination often acts to compound the difficulties they face.

Manchester City is densely populated with approximately 404,000 inhabitants. Thirteen per cent of the respondents of the 1991 census described themselves as Black from African, Asian, Caribbean or Chinese origin. Within the black immigrant population in Manchester, over 6000 head of households were born in the Caribbean (predominantly Jamaica), nearly 5000 were born in Pakistan and 3000 in India. Over 3000 were born in Africa, nearly half in East Africa. The census does not reflect the large population of black people who were born in Great Britain. This has been estimated as nearly 7000 more residents of Manchester who have a grandparent or parent from India, Pakistan, the Caribbean and Africa. Statutory services are increasingly aware of the important part black communities play in Manchester, but they are still not represented in the most influential areas of work, for example as MPs, councillors, senior managers, etc.

The development of the Bibini Centre for Young People

Bibini arose directly from the failure of social care organisations in the statutory and voluntary sector to respond to these conditions. A small group of care-experienced black young people from Manchester attended a conference, Black and In Care, held in London in June 1985. Young black delegates reported to the conference their feelings of isolation, exclusion and alienation. This event inspired the Manchester contingent to continue the struggle back home. They returned determined to develop a support system for themselves in Manchester. Several of the oldest young people approached some black residential workers and social workers they knew and asked them to assist them in establishing the Manchester Black and In Care Group (BIC). The BIC group became a peer support group led by young people providing activities to young people. Many of these aimed to raise black young people's confidence, their understanding of their history and their self-awareness through activities, events and trips during which black young people were able to spend time learning about black culture and gaining emotional support from each other. The Black and in Care group was a direct and practical response to the experience and wishes of these black young people in care. A fundamental feature of the group was the diverse background and experience of the members, as there were Asian, Caribbean, African and black British young people, as well as both disabled and non-disabled regular members.

The fact that the group came from the initiative of black young people created a dynamic for both them and the adults working with them that differed from the more common origins where adults, usually professionals, have taken the initiative. In the early days this profoundly influenced the style of management. The management approach has been to maintain the involvement of young people as central beyond the pioneering stage, including in staff selection and planning the development of the Centre.

Members of the BIC group reported great benefit from meeting each other, especially when they were unable to make contact with their families or black communities, and they quickly recognised some systematic problems in supporting black young people in care. Carers and social care staff regularly undermined arrangements made with young people to attend the group. Messages were not passed on, and it became clear that some white workers did not feel attending the group was a priority for young people. As adults, we discovered that some carers found the prospect of young people in their care attending the group disquieting. Young people were often not transported or staff prioritised other activities over attendance to BIC group. This failure to address the cultural and identity needs of black young people has not changed substantially over the past thirty years (SSI 2000). Very quickly adults in the group had to find ways of tackling the ways that these issues were neglected in the child care system.

As the group developed the adults were greatly disappointed to find that black young people in care were still being placed within culturally mismatched placements and in circumstances that did not meet their cultural needs. We, the adults, were indirectly authorising the placement of black children in isolated circumstances by accepting recommendations for transracial placements with the support of the BIC group. Young people also recognised the limited impact of a social group for black young people in care. A major review was carried out in 1990. The group felt it had not made a sufficient impact through its campaigns to improve services for black young people and identified a need for alternative provision to that currently available through statutory services. The group of young people and adults agreed to explore developing a practical service to provide a range of imaginative holistic services for children that built on the strengths and skills of black individuals and the local black communities.

A young person in the BIC group put forward the suggestion of a children's home for black children. This young man's response to the racism he experienced in his children's home was, 'Why don't we build a home of our own?'. As a result, the BIC Group explored the development of a children's home for black children and young people. This children's home became the Bibini Centre for Young People. The word Bibini means black in a political sense and 'this is really something' in Twi, the language of the Asante people from Ghana, West Africa.

The Bibini Centre for Young People: Our vision and mission

The Bibini Centre was established to challenge racism and discrimination within the care system, to support African, Caribbean, Asian and black British young people in care and empower both black young people and their families.

Adults and young people combined their skills to develop the resource. The Bibini Centre emerged from this collective experience to address the failures in the care system and to provide culturally competent services. Its aims are to:

- provide high-quality residential and community-based services for black young people in or leaving care and those at risk of family break-up

- develop a range of innovative projects which offer practical solutions to the support needs of black young people

- highlight and challenge discrimination and disadvantage within both social care and the wider society.

The Bibini Centre is a wholly independent, registered charity providing holistic child-centred community-based services to black children and young people in care, those leaving care or at risk of family breakdown. The holistic approach we use is recognised in the Department of Health's (2001) Framework for the Assessment of Children but was not mainstream in the early 1990s. Bibini works in an empowering way based on our experience of supporting black young people in care. We provide a range of services within Manchester, but we have a national significance because of our unique service supporting black young people in need.

We have a major role in promoting the improvement of standards within services for black young people and especially those in social care. Challenging discrimination generally and racism specifically is prioritised because it affects black young people and their families. The Bibini Centre has its roots firmly within black communities in Manchester. Among our strengths have been a commitment to community engagement, challenging discrimination, empowering disabled young people and our effectiveness in consulting service users at all stages of our work. The term 'black' is used in a political as well as descriptive sense; it is a unifying term for people subjected to racism on the grounds of racial and cultural origins. In using it we seek to recognise the importance of diversity and difference.

On making the monumental decision to develop a children's home we applied to a range of agencies for funding. The project required skills in management and communication, determination and flexibility. We applied to hundreds of funders, many unsuccessfully, but in two years raised almost £1 million from funders who made a very clear commitment to the organisation's vision. One anonymous donor not only gave a contribution to capital costs but also paid for a development worker post for two years. Adele Jones, now a senior lecturer in social work and Liz Quartey, a social care consultant, were jointly appointed in a developmental role.

Creating a culturally competent children's home

Setting up the children's home for up to eight young people between the ages of 10 and 17 years was not without problems. Planning constraints escalated costs because on the day we were due to start building we learnt that the bricks were not quite the right shade of red. Despite this and the delays it caused we overcame all these problems and difficulties. Local white residents organised petitions to prevent us building a home for black children. Fortunately they were unsuccessful, but we felt that objections were motivated by assumptions that a home for black children in care would result in increased crime and neighbourhood nuisance. This has been totally disproved and some neighbours have become significant supporters, offering young people work experience and advice. This is a result of the efforts we made to provide clear communication and to invite local people to meet the people behind the project.

Becoming inward looking was never an option for the Centre. The surrounding environment has to be a central focus for practice. We defined 'environment' not only as the local community but also the workers and services in statutory, voluntary and private organisations that affected the lives of the young people, their families and black communities. The management of practice had to ensure that all workers took responsibility for contributing to this task because it was integral to promoting young people's life opportunities, and tackling the impact of discrimination staff, young people, their families and communities.

Philosophy

The Bibini Centre for Young People is based on the following principals:

- self-determination
- valuing the diversity of black communities
- challenging racism
- building on the strengths of black people
- helping young people keep their links with families, communities and their local areas
- young people's rights
- challenging discrimination against black disabled young people
- supporting black lesbian and gay young people.

In practice this philosophy fully engages young people and local communities in the developments. Black young people were involved in recruiting the architects and formed a panel for the senior manager's recruitment. This is an excellent opportunity to establish a candidate's ability to communicate with young people and to ensure that young people's views and perspectives are fully recognised. These philosophical aspirations are crucial in devising services to effectively meet the needs of black children and young people by recognising the experience of each individual black child with its family. The aim is to develop a support package which recognises the variety of impacts making up a black young person's identity.

> The aspects of identity and belonging together with needs can provide a good framework from which to capture individual dynamics and work towards a holistic approach to specific services and work with young black people. (Webb 2001)

This methodology provides a useful holistic structure in devising youth projects which can be adapted to the development of other services. The Bibini Centre's commitment to acknowledging and valuing each individual young person's difference enables workers to plan interventions tailored to her or his circumstances and needs. This involves an assessment of each aspect of the young person's experience and celebrates it as a positive contribution to her or his own identity. The manager's role is to support workers, young people and their families in integrating the holistic approach into assessment, planning, services and day-to-day working and living.

Recognizing and adapting to the cultural variety of black communities in Manchester creates a rich and diverse range of services, staff and service users. It makes for a dynamic and innovative environment which in its turn can create management challenges, especially in reconciling a diversity of interests, religions and backgrounds. Services delivered by the Centre are as a result more accessible to previously neglected communities. The approach is consistent with celebrating the skills and resources of black families rather than the negative deficit model used by many statutory and voluntary agencies.

Involvement takes a range of practical forms including the commitment to providing opportunities for service users to influence the delivery of support and development of future services. Young people habitually participate in groups and consultation exercises as do local communities, for example when refugees and asylum seekers joined us to create a steering group for the asylum seekers and refugee project.

The Bibini Centre offers respite and shared care for families caring for children who are challenging. The children's home is registered with the Department of Health and is on most local authority approved lists of service providers. At the beginning the Centre recruited staff who were local people with limited experience of residential care but a range of applicable skills and sympathy to black young people. As time progressed it became clear that the legislation and guidance affecting children's homes required a higher proportion of experienced staff. A Social Services Inspectorate (SSI 2001) report highlighted the challenge of meeting statutory duties and reconciling this with our philosophy of empowerment, particularly in recruitment. A balance has to be struck between demonstrating potential and recruiting staff with experience. We employ staff who are able to 'think out of the box' and create a supportive family environment for black young people. They are also able to engage with young people in a way which has not been possible for white workers because of black workers' greater understanding of black young people's cultural references. There is a common cultural knowledge within black communities, and consequently this can assist staff in developing positive relationships with young people.

Managing innovation and change

The Bibini Centre does not have a static identity. In the process of establishing one service, new needs emerge from analysing the issues raised through our practice and services. The process of developing the residential children's home led to trustees recognising the additional support needs, unmet by current provision in Manchester. Assisting young people about to leave care for the first time brought the recognition of how inappropriate much of the provision available was for black care leavers and led to the development of a supported housing project for black young people. The Leaving Care and Home Project was developed in partnership with Moss Care Housing Association and provides self-contained accommodation and social work support to black young people aged 16 and over who are leaving care, homeless or leaving oppressive housing situations. There are two flats for young people with mobility difficulties and staff support young people with learning disabilities, providing budgeting support, housing advice, and emotional and practical support to all tenants.

The Black Young Carers (BYC) Project resulted from the Trustees' response to a call for a Manchester-wide service for black children and young people with caring responsibilities whose families were touched by a variety of issues including disability, illness and occasionally parents' addiction. As a result of service inadequacies and black families lack of access to them, young people aged from 2 to 25 were undertaking family care responsibilities. The BYC Project's services were used by over one hundred black young people and significantly raised their profile in Manchester for the duration of the Project. It was so successful that statutory services were convinced there was a need to establish a city-wide young carers' service. A hard battle was fought to keep the project specific to black children and young people as some members of the statutory commissioning group wanted to push Bibini into supporting young carers from white communities. Staff and trustees strongly and successfully resisted this. This would not have been possible without a clear philosophy accepted by the whole organisation. The statutory commissioners' then required the successful bidder to secure additional funding. This was a large national charity with a limited track record in supporting local people but substantial funds available to invest.

Learning from the BYC Project developed our experience and commitment to supporting black families holistically, and we went on to create a project for black families in need, the Family Support Service. This has a range of dynamic services working with black families and young people in crisis. Interventions aim to prevent family breakdown, stress and, through support, meet families' collective and individual needs. Project workers provide casework support, advocacy, practical assistance and referrals to other services. The team also recruits volunteers who provide additional assistance. A disability project worker offers support to black disabled people and their families across all of the Bibini Centre projects. The worker also provides advice to staff to assist them raise the profile of disabled young people's experience and needs within social care.

There is a play therapy service providing individual counselling and play therapy to black children and young people who have experienced loss. Some of these young people have had extreme experiences and need to understand and reconcile them with their present circumstances. For example, they may have survived bereavement, war, seeking asylum or the murder of close relatives. Support is also available to children in dealing with relationship breakdown or problems within education.

The Family Support Service more recently developed an asylum seekers and refugee service that provides a range of services to asylum seekers and refugees newly arrived in Britain as well as those more established in Manchester. The worker may be the first port of call for someone who is unfamiliar with the legal and emotional pitfalls involved in seeking asylum and may also require immediate and affective intervention. Advocacy for families has been a crucial role, and within this process it has been important for workers to communicate with many families in their first language. It is amazing to us how few services are able to achieve this standard, for any refugees or indeed families in general. This Family Support Service led to an invitation to manage the new Children's Fund project for asylum seekers, refugee children and their families. The partnership also includes Save the Children, Manchester Ethnic Minority Achievement Service and Refugee Aid. This new city-wide service will be line managed by the Family Support Services manager.

The Bibini Centre currently provides services to around one hundred and thirty black young people from the age of 6 and 25, including disabled young people. The children and young people using our service come from diverse backgrounds and have complex needs. We are working with families who originate from Pakistan, Sudan, India, Monserrat, Somalia, Nigeria and the Caribbean as well as black British and mixed-parentage families. We also support families whose religious backgrounds include Christian, Muslim and Rastafarian faiths. Some of the young people are particularly isolated and have become alienated from their communities, and here we work to re-establish contact with their families or develop further links within local black communities. The management of practice has to routinely work to maintain these networks that are crucial to the identity and positive outcomes for the young people using the Centre.

Residential care is provided to young people from anywhere in the country, from both urban and rural authorities. We have cared for young people from local authorities as diverse as London, Birmingham, Sheffield, Cheshire, Liverpool, Manchester and Stockport. We offer training and consultancy services and conference presentations as well as workshops to national, local and regional events. Local children and those from Greater Manchester predominantly use our other community-based services. Our local and national work gives us a foundation of practical experience to offer other agency support and advice in working with black young people and to identify gaps in service provision.

Working holistically means that the shape of services and the skills of the workers in them have had to be tailored to the needs of the young people, their families and communities. Managers have to acquire the ability to manage mixed-skill teams rather than remaining in the safety of their own professional expertise. We have successfully promoted a culture in which staff value the support other professionals provide to young people that promotes their health, education and their life opportunities. Members of these teams have had to learn to value each other's contribution and to ensure that they have access to support in their own area of expertise. External inspection has acknowledged the way that staff are supportive of each other in what is a difficult task and that training is provided to ensure a consistent approach to children and young people (Social Services Inspectorate 2001).

Our passage through these changes has not always been easy, and we, like many others, have experienced difficulties in recruitment and from staff changes. Having a clear mission, and recruiting staff who are very clear about the task and a culture of listening to and working with young people, have enabled us, as a group and with our trustees, to address these issues in a constructive way and to avoid a blame culture.

Each time we have considered establishing a new service we have drawn on our own expertise combined with that of the young people, their families and communities and existing research into the experience of black children and families. When this has been either partial or insufficient we have undertaken our own research and recently completed a research project on black young people's experience of homelessness. The Bibini Centre also undertook a two-year study examining the circumstances of black young people, how they become homeless, what services they use and how they feel services can be made more appropriate. Black professionals must reclaim research into black communities to ensure that our history is accurately and impartially recorded.

Inequalities in the access to services

The founders of the Bibini Centre were well aware of the impact of discrimination on black service users, especially in their relationships with statutory agencies. In the 1980s these experiences were confirmed by, for example, the Commission for Racial Equality, which found evidence that Tower Hamlets LB (CRE 1988) used the criteria of 'priority needs', 'intentionality' and 'local connection' in defining homelessness to discriminate against ethnic minority homeless and evade their statutory duties. Poor housing remains an issue at the beginning of the twenty-first century. The Bibini Centre's experience has been that insecure housing, economic hardship and a greater level of unemployment in black communities put additional stresses on families who are already living with racism and discrimination. The physical conditions can result in damp, cold and environmental dangers such as carbon monoxide build-up, and overcrowding is an issue for many low-income black families. This can cause a disintegration of relationships, lack of privacy and resultant mental health problems. The management issues in this situation are complex; workers need to be supported in their challenging and advocacy roles for black families, especially when negotiating with statutory agencies.

The family support team has regularly assisted families to over come housing need, secure improved housing and, on two occasions, to negotiate rehousing after the family house had been condemned. Black young people interviewed as part of the Centre's research study on housing reported their negative experiences of becoming homeless and dissatisfaction in the provision available to them. They were generally alienated from statutory services, and when hostel support became available it was felt to be unsuitable to the needs of the black young people placed there.

> It was horrible. I don't want to be ungrateful or anything but, it was smelly. I was in accommodation for a family, which was not satisfactory. The cutlery was dirty. I had to clean the place from scratch. You should see the state of the pans. The neighbours had dogs, which made it smell. There were beetles, and insects – large big thick ones. (Asian female, 29 years old, quoted in Baxter, Baxter and Baxter 2001)

As one-mixed parentage (Caribbean and white) young woman said, 'nothing was good, but I suppose at least I was not outside' (Baxter *et al.* 2001). Current service provision is inadequate and does not take into account the cultural needs of young people (Steele 1997). Repeatedly black young people are at the end of the queue in service development and delivery.

In contrast, the services offered within black projects such as the Bibini Centre have highlighted their potential to black young people. For example, a partnership, developed with a housing drop-in service for black young people, drew black young people into organisations they were unaware of, or projects they had previously felt were not accessible to them. The drop-in facilitates a more direct method of communication between generic health service providers and young people. Dedicated service delivery plays a crucial part in ensuring black young people have equal access to services. The Bibini Centre believes that the development of dedicated services can have a positive impact on generic services by leading the way in access issues, monitoring and meeting the needs of specific black communities. Managers of successful black projects have ensured that service and practice development is flexible enough by tailoring them to the holistic and specific needs of the black communities they serve.

Ill health of young people and their families makes a significant impact on the well-being of black children and young people. Significant differences exist in the experience of ill health between black communities and the general population of the UK. Black communities in general have shorter life expectancy and poorer physical and mental health than the white population. Black and ethnic minority groups in the North West also experience 30 per cent more hospitalisations than the general population (NHS North West Regional Office 1996). Ill health can create pressures on the whole circumstances of black families, including financial strains, as is particularly evident from our work with black young people with caring re-sponsibilities. Bibini Centre managers are concerned that reduced access to preventative health services and health information create the increased level of morbidity experienced by black communities. Black people's anger has acted as a catalyst to black health and welfare groups, such as the Bibini Centre, to develop more accessible health services.

Culturally competent practice and services

The Bibini Centre developed services which take these societal impacts into account. The disproportionate experience of poverty leaves black families barred from many aspects of society and excluded from statutory services. Many black families receiving support from the Bibini Centre found themselves unable to secure the support they need or felt deeply suspicious and reluctant to engage with white agencies. They were concerned that they would experience racism when requesting assistance, or had previously experienced discrimination when approaching appropriate statutory services. Our study into the needs of black young people with caring responsibilities found that parents' concerns that they would be perceived negatively was a major barrier to seeking services and support from social services (Jones, Jeyasingham and Rajasooriya 2001). This study confirmed the experience of the Family Support Service and the BYC Project before it. A distinctive feature of both of these was that we also supported families in dealing with the impacts of racism. Front-line staff's practice can demonstrate generalisations and misunderstandings of black people. Aspects of the Victoria Climbié tragedy (Laming 2003) at the time of writing not being discussed widely, are the stereotypical assumptions about an African child and the child's family by professionals attempting to protect Victoria and the fact that black workers can make assumptions as a result of a lack of knowledge. There is a potential for inaccurate assessment and stereo-typing when African parents are perceived as overbearing, Caribbean families as chaotic, Asian families look after their own, etc. Examination of the true relationships and personalities does not take place.

At the Bibini Centre managers and staff constantly need to be aware of stereotypes and able to recognise them as they arise. When agencies fail to provide appropriate services and fail to enable black families to secure support, this can compound assumptions made about black service users. In contrast, external inspection of the Centre recognised the way that staff provide positive role models for the young people from diverse backgrounds and cultures and that young people's cultural heritage is integrated into planning for their future (SSI 2001).

As black families do not feel able to request help from social services they are often invisible to professionals and have to utilise their own resources. Many black young carers interviewed experienced a higher level of respon-sibility in the family than white young carers. They were also expected to act as interpreters for their relatives during interviews with health and welfare professionals and sometimes to be 'cultural interpreters', explaining religious, cultural and family norms, to unaware white professionals. Black young carers' representatives had a clear responsibility in advocating on behalf of black families. This included challenging service providers, for example, when health staff released an extremely sick father into the care of his 15-year-old daughter but were unwilling to discuss his medication regime with her. One young carer told us:

> People at school and from my community thought and said it was part of my culture in fact everyone said that this is what we do – look after others. I never had a choice – nurses came to see my mum and it was like I was not there. I do not mind doing what I do – I just wish I had a say ... More Young Carers Projects need to be established that meet all cultural needs – it is good to have someone out of the family to talk to. (*On Reflection* 2001)

The manager of the Family Support Service recognised the difficulty for black young people to reconcile their need to be children and young people, as well as to express their significant levels of responsibility. As a result the services and practice encourage young people to in explore all aspects of their experience, from support for studying to social activities.

Our model of intervention

The model of our intervention at the Black Young Carers Project was developed as a specific attempt to empower and enable families in their own circumstances. This approach makes children's and parental rights central in the negotiation of supporting families. In addition there is an understanding that support sometimes takes the form of more formal intervention, which can be unwelcome, especially with regards to child protection responsibilities. Organisational policy is that discussions about child protection are open and the families are kept fully informed. They know they can be confident that workers would not undertake referrals or investigation without their knowledge. This creates a level of trust which is often not evident in their relationships with other agencies. Black communities' access to statutory services will only improve when they consult and engage in partnerships with black workers and black community projects as these are the people black individuals' turn to when they are in need. Generic service providers must examine their services dispassionately and learn from the experiences of more specialist agencies.

The Bibini Centre continues to have a firm commitment to supporting black children and young people in care. The black and in care worker has created a network for black young people in care and is supporting young people in the creation of a forum for young people in care, including young people in residential care, foster care or placed at home. This forum is led by the young people and aims to help them in gaining confidence and social skills. The worker also assists residential care staff to create effective care packages for black children and young people in their care by giving practical advice such as the implications of religious observance, food preparation and care needs or training staff to better understand black young people. Young people involved in the project are in the process of creating a drama presentation and will be developing a website for black young people in care.

There were 6300 children and young people in children's homes at the 31 March 1999: 4800 were placed in community homes, 500 in voluntary homes and 1000 in private registered homes (Department of Health 2000). In the main, social services departments have yet to instigate cultural monitoring across services, but the Government intends that the population of black young people be researched and fully established. It is hard to imagine how social services departments can effectively parent black young people when they are unclear about where they live or their cultural background. This reinforces the importance of effective monitoring of young people's ethnicity and the ability to examine their experience in care. For the last fifty years black children and young people have been overrepresented within the care population, particularly those of Caribbean or mixed Caribbean and white parentage (Barn *et al.* 1997; Bebbington and Miles 1989; Fitzherbert 1967; Pinder and Shaw 1974).

Staff at the Bibini Centre have to understand why parents might need to place their black children and young people into care in order to provide non-judgemental support. By understanding the extreme pressures on black family life we can see the political analysis in an individual's situation. Many professionals and agencies, prior to working with us, have often failed black young people. Residential staff need understanding that young people are likely to be suspicious of staff and unclear about our motivation, and they may not have spent significant time with black people before. Families may also feel concerned that their child is living with black people, especially if they themselves have internalised views of black people as being unprofessional and unreliable. Staff have to overcome these stereotypes because where parenrs hold these views, they will have been passed on to young people. As a result it often feels that our work has to be better and more open to scrutiny than elsewhere and this is a constant issue for black managers when they are managing practice and quality standards at the same time as resisting unrealistic and sometimes unfair expectations of black staff.

As innovators the Bibini Centre learns from all possible areas of advice and experience, especially from other black run organisations that continue to grow as a response to the inappropriate provision of some services which excludes black service users and communities. In effectively managing a black project, black managers need to consider how to reconcile the needs of service users, staff and external impacts on the black organisation.

The Black voluntary sector

No one in a black organisation can ignore the fact that they work in the black voluntary sector because it forms part of the context for practice. The rise of black and ethnic minority housing associations (EMHA) created the predecessors and models for black social care organisations. The earliest EMHAs were founded in the 1960s and 1970s without special support and were relatively small in size. Black-run organisations share several of these difficulties to this day. They are unevenly disturbed geographically; many are concentrated in London and the larger cities and have a less secure financial base compared to mainstream organisations. This is in part a consequence of size and of being relatively recent, and also of the impact of generalisations, discrimination and stereotyping which is particularly evident in many areas of contact with external agencies. Lattimer (1991) evaluates the views and values of funding bodies towards ethnic minority organisations. The overwhelming approach adopted by trusts was a colour-blind approach, with 80 per cent of funders believing that ethnic minority status should be disregarded when considering applications. This fails to recognise the impact of discrimination, or institutional racism, and as a result there are no strategies to ensure equal access by facilitating applications from black groups and organisations. The Bibini Centre's experience is that some funders require a higher level of information, accountability and assessment from black voluntary agencies than for the wider voluntary sector. Some of our funding applications have been examined with what seems to be suspicion and antipathy. At times additional referees have been required, or external experts engaged to reassure funders. This is not unique to the Bibini Centre. In the consultation exercise by the Home Office of black voluntary agencies

> The main problems nowadays for many black and ethnic minority voluntary organisations are the suspicion and insensitivity they encounter in public bodies and the wider voluntary sector. They feel for example that they have to operate under greater scrutiny from funders. This has sometimes led to mistrust between white managed funding bodies and black minority ethnic voluntary organisations. (Home Office 1999)

Bibini has been largely unable to secure rolling contracts from statutory services and has had to rely on spot purchasing. The current trend of funding organisations that already have contracts will probably lead to awards given to the larger, more established and mainly white organisations (Lattimer 1991). Since black and minority ethnic groups are underrepresented as users of statutory services these decisions will further entrench the racial inequalities. One-off funding creates greater financial instability and an over dependence on statutory services. The Family Rights Group undertook an overview of services available to black and ethnic minority children and the views of representatives from black voluntary agencies. Many respondents report that lip service was paid by statutory agencies to culturally appropriate services involving voluntary agencies.

> Yes we are known, and we've had referrals, although it's a token gesture. Say there's a family who might want to adopt a black child and they think that if you buy into this group, that's addressing these issues. So we've had foster carers who've come along because Social Services said it would be a good idea to, but we've never had any meaningful contact with anybody. But it helps them to feel they've addressed the issues. (FRG 1989)

This piecemeal approach does not facilitate effective service planning and consistency in support of black children and young people. Service users greatly benefit from statutory services developing partnerships and service agreements with black voluntary organisations or community groups. Unfortunately these arrangements are fraught with difficulties, and the power dynamics create a situation where the black voluntary agency can feel dominated by the funders and larger organisation. Black voluntary agencies can be drawn into the politics of statutory services, especially when funding is offered to one voluntary organisation at the cost of another. A minority of funding policy makers and commissioning officers encourage competition between groups in the hope that competing groups will motivate lower costs or efficiencies as opposed to promoting partnerships. Sometimes information about grants is not widely distributed and black organisations do not get notification of funding rounds, or forums, where priorities are likely to be discussed.

All those involved in negotiating agreements and front line staff who will be affected by the decision have to be fully aware of the philosophical aims of the project and the organisation's bottom line. The burden for establishing this position all too often falls on the black voluntary organisation and the struggle they have 'to make their case' can lead to a view that they are 'difficult to work with' rather than that they are effective in providing culturally appropriate services. The alternative is that many voluntary agencies are diverted from their aim or objectives as a result of offers of funding. The lesson from our experience is that one size does not fit all.

The context for managers of practice includes experiencing racism and discrimination against themselves as individuals and towards their staff or the users of the service, shortage of funds, and the general requirement to advocate for those who are the least powerful in our society. A key message which has arisen as a result of the development of specialist services, from the work of the Bibini Centre for Young People is that it is important to engage and involve the full range of black communities in the design of support projects. Front line staff have to concentrate on the individual needs of black families and to consult with the young people who are likely to become service users of the project. Within the development and delivery of services it has been crucial for the differences and experiences of black communities not only to be acknowledged but also catered for.

Black managers have to negotiate the competing requirements of black communities and staff, and are to be the most flexible of practitioners. Many of the issues experienced by all managers of practice are the same, however in a black agency they have also to reconcile the demands of the service users and the impact of discrimination on the organisation and the individuals within it. This creates the challenges inherent in delivering services from a new community-based perspective. It also creates the satisfaction of working within an organisation with a strong mandate from community groups and allows the freedom of individuals to express themselves.

References

Barn, R., Sinclair, R. and Ferdinand, D. (1997) *Acting on Principle: An Examination of Race and Ethnicity in Social Services Provision for Children and Families.* London: British Association of Adoption and Fostering.

Baxter, D. Jnr, Baxter, L. and Baxter, C. (2001) 'Young Homeless and Black in Manchester.' Unpublished. The Bibini Centre for Young People.

Bebbington, A. and Miles, J. (1989) 'The Background of Children who Enter Care.' *British Journal of Social Work 19*, 349–68.

CRE (Commission for Racial Equality) (1988) *Homelessness and Discrimination. Report into the London Borough of Tower Hamlets.* London: CRE.

Department of Health, Department for Education and Employment and the Home Office (2001) *Framework for the Assessment of Children in Need and their Families.* London: HMSO.

Fitzherbert, K. (1967) *West Indian Children in London.* London: Croom Helm.

Home Office (1999) *Strengthening the Black and Minority Ethnic Voluntary Sector Infrastructure.* London: HMSO.

Jones, A., Jeyasingham, D. and Rajasooriya, S. (2001) *Invisible families: The Strengths and Needs of Black Families in which Young People have Caring Responsibilities.* Bristol: Policy Press.

Karn, V. (1997) '"Ethnic penalties" and Racial Discrimination in Education, Employment and Housing: Conclusions and policy implications.' Ch. 13 in V. Karn (ed) *Employment, Education and Housing Amongst Ethnic Minorities in Britain: Ethnicity in the 1991 Census, vol 4.* London: ONS.

Laming, Lord (2003) *The Victoria Climbié Inquiry: Report of an Inquiry.* London: The Stationery Office.

Lattimer, M. (1991) The funding of black and ethnic minority groups. London: HMSO.

Manchester Management Action Plan (2001) 'Manchester Social Services.' Unpublished.

North West Regional Office (1996) *Small Area Database: Hospital Activity.* January.

On Reflection (2001) *The Bibini Centre for Young People's First Year Review.* Manchester.

Peach, C. (1996) 'Does Britain Have Ghettos?' *Transactions Institute of British Geographers 21,* 1, 216–35.

Pinder, R. and Shaw, M. (1974) 'Coloured Children in Long Term Care.' Unpublished report, University of Leicester, School of Social Work.

Richards, A. and Ince, L. (1989) *Overcoming the Obstacles: Looked After Children: Quality Services for Black and Ethnic Minority Children and their Families.* London: Family Rights Group.

SSI (Social Services Inspectorate) (2000) *Excellence Not Excuses.* London: Department of Health.

SSI (Social Services Inspectorate) (2001) *Inspection of the Bibini Centre for Young People, Voluntary Children's Home.* London: Local Inspection Report, Department of Health.

Steele, A. (1997) *Young Drifting and Black: A Report on the Findings and Recommendations of a Study into Young Black Homelessness for the Nottingham City Council.* Nottingham: Nottingham City Council.

Webb, M. (2001) 'Black Young People.' In *The Russell House Publishing Companion to Working with Young People.* Lyme Regis, Dorset: Russell House.

CHAPTER 5

Supervision and Governance

Gerardine Cunningham

In Northern Ireland health and social care services are already combined at the local level and clinical and social care governance requirements have applied to social care also in recent times. The Government in Northern Ireland has incorporated into the statutory duties of health and social services trusts the responsibility for ensuring 'high quality clinical care'. Chief executives are held responsible for the quality of practice as well as the use of resources, and there must be mechanisms in place to assure them that quality care is indeed being offered. This chapter describes how the Ulster Community and Hospitals Trust brought this agenda into social work. This was greatly facilitated by work that the Trust had already undertaken on standards of practice in social work (Smythe, Simmons and Cunningham 1999). Professional supervision is a mechanism already in place within social work that can contribute to the Trust ensuring clinical and social care governance and continuing professional development of staff. Supervision lends itself to quality assurance and governance, and the achievement of best practice.

The NHS definition of clinical governance is 'A framework which NHS organisations are accountable for continuously improving the quality of their services and safeguarding high standards of care by creating an environment in which excellence in clinical care will flourish' (NHS 1998). The language used to convey the concept of governance has been overlain with health and medical imagery, and in the early days the policy on governance was of 'clinical governance'. Full credit must be given to the medical and nursing professions, who have embraced the concept and indeed have created models for measuring the quality of clinical interventions. By 2002 documents such as *The Employer of Choice* (DHSSPS 2002) and *Best Practice, Best Care* (DHSSPS 2001) have laid down the challenge for best practice achievable through the governance agenda. It would be fair to say that social work/social care has been engaged in some of the activities of governance before this policy was developed, but in the past the supervision function was not framed within a systematic approach to accountability. Within the Ulster Community and Hospitals Trust we have travelled some distance on the clinical governance journey through the development of a standards and audit approach. The work has been developed over a period of some seven years and it took this length of time to embed the system throughout the organisation, particularly within the expectations of practitioners, managers and people using services. The system is open and explicit and therefore can be both challenged and changed by these different stakeholders in the Trust and its services. This has been achieved by the publication of the book *Quality Assurance in Social Work* (Smyth, Simmons and Cunningham 1999) which describes the process of developing standards and the methods of audit which can be used to assure quality practice.

We have identified professional supervision as the natural vehicle for ensuring measurement, accountability and quality of practice. We also recognised that having come out of a general management era, there was a necessity to enable the team leader role to regain the management of practice element which had been eroded in the previous decade, as the governance agenda places the professional firstline management role as a key watchdog for social work practice.

Smyth, Simmons and Cunningham undertook this work within the Ulster Community and Hospitals Trust as a consequence of being commissioned by the Department of Health to test the feasibility of standard setting across social work staff. This project engaged with social workers, managers and service users to define standards which represented the work of social workers. This was then developed into a tool which was practice based and thus provided social workers themselves, and line managers, with a mechanism for reflection and feedback.

At the time, 1995–99, this work predated the governance agenda. However, because standards and audit became part of the social work culture within the Trust, there was a readiness for the acceptance of governance when it arrived.

Mike McCullagh (2001) has offered a very helpful model that sets out the key components of clinical governance as they relate to the primary care setting in Ipswich that can be adapted for social care. The components of the model that are relevant to social care are:

- establishing a learning culture

- supporting and applying evidence-based practice

- accountability and performance

- risk management

- improving health

- quality improvement systems, including clinical audit

- establishing a research and development culture

- involvement of patients and the public.

All of these components are compatible with trends within social work and social care. Table 5.1 illustrates how this is achieved.

The table demonstrates how the concepts of clinical governance are very much embedded within the supervisory system for social work. This is highly significant in implementing the change agenda required because it demonstrates that social work has already taken major steps to meet governance requirements, albeit unconsciously. Since the introduction of community care legislation through People First (1991) in Northern Ireland, social workers moved from a therapeutic focus to a task-centred focus as the legislation and policy created a preoccupation with the delivery of services. In this environment reflection on practice is not a natural part of the process as we lend ourselves to practices, which can be mechanistic.

Table 5.1: The correlation between clinical and social care governance	
Clinical Governance	Social Care Governance
Establishing a learning culture	Lifelong learning continuum – NVQ – Professional Qualification – Post Qualifying Award – Advanced Award
Supporting and applying evidence-based practice	Identifying models of intervention – getting the right model for the right situation
Accountability and performance	Supervision
Risk management	Assessment and management of risk in terms of vulnerability and protection Protection plans which directly address vulnerability
Quality improvement systems (including clinical audit).	• working to standards • file audit • direct observation • supervision
Establishing a research and development culture	Since Children's Order, greater use of legal precedents, best practice research A research base is beginning to be built regarding vulnerable adults, domestic violence, community development
Involvement of patients and the public	Service user involvement in: • assessments • individual planning • service development • policy development • complaints • working groups re problem solving • mentoring and role modelling for other service users

The first work of the standards was to refocus social workers on what the nature of practice was and to help the move back to a more analytical approach. This resulted in the expectation that social workers would be able to explain, and justify what they do, to managers, people using services and to their profession as part of accountable practice which identifies the linkage between process and therapeutic outcomes. This is a time for moving from instinct to conscious evaluation of what we are doing that already locates social work and professional supervision firmly in the governance frame.

In the work which was carried out by Smyth, Simmons and Cunningham, the introduction of standards and audit was perceived by all as a time-limited project and, while there was clear interest, it was seen as an additional piece of work.

The audit function was initially carried out by the training and development team, but this resulted in trainers becoming the experts in good practice and poor practice with no mandate to challenge the poor practice through the continuous loop of feedback, available through supervision. The best that could be achieved was that practice trends could be fed through to line managers.

The work in the Trust has persisted through working with the first-line managers to help them see audit as a mechanism for feedback and ensuring the achievement of good practice as standard. This effort has been worthwhile, as the emergence of clinical governance has found a receptive culture within the social work profession.

Supervision as the vehicle for Governance

Kadushin (1976) was one of the main interpreters of supervision within the social work setting. He argues that supervision contains three main components:

- the supportive role
- the education role
- the management role.

Proctor supports this three-way split using the terms formative, restorative and normative (Hawkins and Shohet 2000).

Supportive function

The supportive/restorative function is an acknowledgement on the part of the manager that engagement in therapeutic work affects the social worker because he or she is working on an ongoing basis with people's pain. Within supervision, workers must have space to be restored and given time to unburden themselves of the trauma of painful encounters in order to go back into similar situations and continue to work effectively. The supportive function therefore takes on a debriefing role.

Educative function

The educative/formative function is 'developing the skills, understanding and abilities' of staff. Hawkins and Shohet (2000) go on to say that this should enable the worker to:

- 'understand the client better;
- become more aware of their own reactions and responses to the client;
- understand the dynamics of how they and their client were interacting;
- look at how they intervened and the consequences of their intervention;
- explore other ways of working with this; and other similar client situations.'

This emphasises the need for reflection on practice to be very much part of the supervision encounter. It requires the worker and the supervisor to separate out what went well and what hindered, and brings social work theory and methods on to the supervision agenda. Supervision uses reflection on direct practice as a method for professional learning by eliciting the explanations and the evidence on which assessments and interventions were based. A result of this process is that workers and their managers are first able to articulate for themselves and then communicate to people using services what has underpinned their assessments and their choice of interventions. Professional supervision provides the mechanism for workers to be accountable to people using services as well as to management as part of governance.

Management function

The managerial or normative function 'provides a quality control function in work with people' in order to help look at 'blind spots, areas of vulnerability from our own wounds and our prejudices' (Hawkins and Shohet 2000). This overseeing function ensures that standards within agencies are being met and that service users, regardless of which worker responds, are getting the same service and have the same opportunity for increased well-being. To do this the supervisor must actively acquaint himself or herself with not only the tasks the worker has completed but also the how and why of the worker's practice. The management role is to identify inconsistencies in practice and to challenge poor practice, to identify best practice and to create opportunities for sharing and celebration. It is this latter role that has in the past been forgotten too often. We see social workers chided for what they have done wrong but rarely celebrated for what they have done right.

Governance incorporates the managerial and educative functions explicitly.

In order to use supervision as a mechanism for governance the supervisor must establish a learning culture for the team and the individual so that skills are updated and models of intervention reviewed on a regular basis. This is consistent with the investigation into the death of Frederick Joseph McLernon, where the educative function was clearly reinforced: 'Line managers should ensure that supervision applies the principles of social work and relevant theoretical knowledge' (DHSS 1998). This means that the line manager must know about the different theories and methods, and their application in different contexts. In order to use the supervision session as an opportunity for modelling and coaching they need to have some expectations as to which methods of intervention work in certain situations. If this training activity is present within the supervision session it creates immediacy by offering an opportunity to correct practice more quickly. This approach concurs with Shulman's (1999) advice that it is not about never making a mistake but, rather, is about lessening the time between making the mistake and catching the mistake.

This does not need to be restricted to individual supervision, but also can be expanded to the team meeting, which can be used as a method of group supervision. This increases the opportunities for feedback from peers and thus enhance the learning opportunities.

This educative function also encompasses evidence-based practice – practice that is underpinned by knowledge and models of intervention which are known to work and, if applied across similar circumstances, will produce a successful outcome. The following are examples of this:

- The successful application of the Egan model of counselling which has successfully enabled people to move from their present and past scenarios to their preferred scenarios (Egan 1990).

- The use of group work where a number of clients share a similar concern, which requires support and strength from a common identity. In the Trust successful examples of these are the carers support groups and the service users consultation group.

- The community development model where the community and neighbourhood is targeted on removing barriers and building capacity to include individuals who would otherwise be socially excluded. This is consistent with the Systems model (Pincus and Minahan 1973) that moves the focus of practice away from the client system alone to the target system that can be external to the service user.

All of these models are social work pathways in the same way that doctors use models of treatment, i.e., prescribing medication, surgery, radiotherapy, etc. Social work managers and social workers must value their interventions and their capacity to alleviate emotional pain with the same confidence as other professionals.

Governance is an opportunity for social workers to regain their evidence base and, in a focused and disciplined way, engage service users in the healing process. Research underpins the educative function as it complements evidence-based practice and provides empirical evidence of effectiveness or ineffectiveness. This has been a long-neglected area of social work. Governance requirements help to maintain evidence-based practice on the agenda and will as a result encourage research which will promote the benefits of social work.

Supervision, governance and quality assurance

Some of the key areas of governance fit very easily into the managerial function of supervision, for example:

- accountability and performance
- risk management
- quality improvement and audit
- service user involvement.

Accountability

The qualified worker has to be accountable to professional standards and to the organisation through its management arrangements. The mechanism of supervision must demonstrate accountability through the supervisor's capacity to evaluate and monitor performance. At the same time as providing information to the organisation the supervisor gives feedback to the workers when they have carried out best practice and also when identifying blind spots that need to be addressed. The McLernon Report (DHSS 1998) endorses this: 'Line managers should ensure that supervision is used to examine practice and identify issues, which the worker may have missed' (DHSS 1998).

Feedback is important to growth as well as safety. Feedback can be seen as criticism, and the worker can become defensive. The role of professional feedback in maintaining a culture of learning within the team has to be established during the worker's induction period. Everyone needs to understand that feedback is part of the supervision process to provide support and protection for the worker and the organisation. Workers can then feel safer in soliciting feedback, rather than being passive receivers, because they understand that this will strengthen both accountability and professional development.

Risk assessment

A key part of accountability in terms governance and professional practice is risk assessment. Risk assessment and risk management have always been readily identifiable as management tasks within social work, particularly within family and child care work in terms of child protection. Risk management is also an important facet in working with adults, as protection of vulnerable adults is now underpinned by policy and supported by current domestic violence legislation. The management function in relation to risk management is strongly endorsed by the McLernon Report, which states: 'In situations of potential/actual risk, line managers should ensure that a formal assessment of risk is carried out' (DHSS 1998).

Within the Ulster Community and Hospital Trust, social work risk assessment follows the Brearley Model that looks at the history of hazards with a view to predicting likelihood of reoccurrence (Brearley 1982). Documentation is systematic and designed as a pathway which should lead the worker through good practice. The model has used a systems approach with information gathered from all significant people in the service user's social network. The outcome is a robust document which facilitates information gathering and analysis from which more accurate decision making is possible. The Trust's document was constructed by two first-line managers, piloted and amended on the basis of feedback from the social workers from the elderly and physical disability programmes. It is therefore grounded in social work practice, supports the social worker by providing a framework for their work and provides the information supervisors need to be accountable to the organisation and the service user.

The policy of the Trust is that all documentation should outline best practice. This has been a helpful construct learned from the 'care pathway' movement within medical and nursing professions. The principle is that documentation should be designed in such a way that the best practice approach is logically represented within documentation so that the same quality can be offered to all clients, rather than depending on the innovativeness of the practitioner.

The first line managers are responsible for periodically reviewing documentation to ensure that it is fit for purpose and in line with current good practice and to ensure that changes are made as policy, theory and research findings challenge present practices.

Our evaluation is that within the elderly and physical disability programmes practice in risk assessment has improved with the introduction of pathway-led documentation.

Quality assurance and audit

The management function within supervision should also include issues of quality through the audit process. Some concepts around audit, taken from various dictionaries, are:

- inspection
- correction
- verification
- certification.

These are fundamental to social work, and whereas in the past these functions may have rested in the domain of external agencies, in the Ulster Community and Hospitals Trust we have asked the first line manager to take responsibility for the first three. Practice audit has become part of the supervisory system. It is the means through which practice is overseen and scrutinised (inspected), and feedback is given (correction or congratulations) and verified as fit for purpose. The certification stage comes about when the line manager enables the social worker to make the link from supervised practice to post qualifying (PQ) or advanced level accreditation.

It is our preference within the Trust to have the line manager as an active member of the PQ candidate's support system. Managers align PQ with the audit process and actively observe practice. They have the opportunity to scrutinise more closely the cases the worker is using as evidence, to become familiar with the theories and models of intervention being used, and to ensure these continue to be used in day-to-day practice after the worker has achieved his or her PQ accreditation. The line manager acts as a mechanism for consolidating learning and professional development within the workplace. This role for the line manager as actively involved in the certification of practice will be further confirmed with the advent of the Northern

Ireland Social Care Council where the line manager will be involved in endorsing the registration and re-registration of staff members.

Audit is also understood as a cyclical activity, which leads to continuous improvement through the use of standards and audit of standards against practice (see Figure 5.1).

The audit cycle is useful in that it helps the manager move through a systematic reviewing process and to know at any one time what the strengths and weaknesses are within the team, and it is therefore useful for identifying training more accurately.

A standards and audit approach gives line managers more accurate information about the state of practice in their team. By being able to locate problems either in systems or practice they are able to make better training and management decisions.

The Ulster Community and Hospitals Trust have been leaders in the field of writing occupational standards for social work. The existence of standards does not ensure quality or improvements in practice. It is only when practice is audited against standards that there is true knowledge of the state of practice.

Taylor and Devine (1993) state that information is only useful if it is retrievable. Within social work, knowledge is contained in two main areas: (1) on the pages within the file; and (2) in the heads of social workers. It is the line manager's job through supervision and audit to make sense of all the information contained on pages and in heads of social workers and convert it into an understanding of the

- level of practice competence
- quality of service users' experience
- added value which a competent workforce brings to both service users and the Trust.
- staff training needs which are real rather than aspirational
- fitness of documentation for purpose
- supportiveness for the professional task of organisational systems.

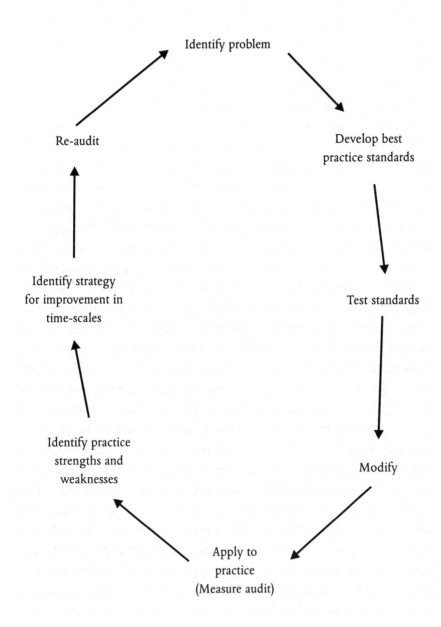

Figure 5.1 The audit cycle

An abundance of initiatives accost the workforce, for example the TOPSS training strategy, Charter Mark, Health Quality Service (HQS), multi-professional audit, clinical governance. Staff feel confused and burdened. Like a loom with only the vertical threads in place there is a collection of individual strands with little or no understanding as to how these initiatives can be mutually supportive in achieving the same outcomes. Yet, within a coherent framework, PQ can be a route to identifying and celebrating best practice and the same evidence used for quality awards, i.e., the Charter Mark and HQS. This in turn contributes towards a systematic approach to clinical governance. Line managers can help bring all these strands together to enable both individuals and the team to achieve service awards. From these horizontal strands the line managers can create the fabric of good practice.

The Trust decided to bring these different strands of auditing practice together. Having been at the forefront of developing social work standards (Smyth, Simmons and Cunningham 1999) and being part of the HQS Accreditation it seemed natural to attempt to match social work standards with HQS expectations so that we could help staff achieve compliance in both without additional effort and duplication. We met with the National Institute for Social Work and HQS to find a way of incorporating the social work standards into the HQS assessment process. The standards were put into HQS format, which focused on systems, practices, policies and procedures, and challenged the propensity for reliance on custom and practice with which we are comfortable within social work. The result clearly showed how much we assumed practices were in place because we had always done things that way. Custom and practice (the inheritance of good practice culture through an experienced workforce) rather than written policies and guidance work well when there is a stable workforce. However, in a time of scarcity and fluidity in the social work workforce there is dilution of the age-old wisdom which results in arbitrariness rather than standardisation. Another danger in the inheritance of received wisdom is that there is an assumption that it is actually good practice. However, we have to continuously incorporate new legislation, policies, methods of intervention, and what was acceptable twenty years ago may be no longer relevant.

For the purposes of piloting the joint HQS and social work standards the methodology we used was file audit. Previously, when we audited the social work standards in their original form with a pure practice focus, there was evidence of best practice in the assessment stages of work with clients but improvements were needed in the planning process. When we applied the HQS formated social work standards with the incorporation of systems and processes it showed clearly a deficit in the documentation, which only asked for an initial plan rather than a long-term plan. The result was that workers found it difficult to focus on long-term planning. A system fault was responsible for a practice weakness. This helped managers make the appropriate changes in the documentation and thus manage the practice quality.

The information gleaned from file audits ought to enable line managers to formulate the right questions, to help practitioners to reflect on their practice. This should also align with the PQ core competence of reflective practice. The audit helped first line managers to make sense of the information found on files and to see how the organisational systems either helped or hindered practice. This shows that audit can assist with problem-solving.

Service user involvement

No quality assurance process is complete without the involvement of service users on a micro and macro basis. All assessments must be shared with, and agreed by, the service user as he or she must be regarded as the expert in their own lives. We have consulted with service users on all policies, including the audit. One important lesson from this work is that policies must be written in accessible language rather than 'policy-speak'.

Service users have made important contributions to service development within the physical disability programme, particularly on the implementation of direct payments. The Trust was able to facilitate the service users receiving direct payments to compile a practice guide for other service users on how to manage a direct payment. This was professionally published and has led to service users being invited to be consultants in training events with staff.

One of the main results of working so closely with service users on implementing the direct payment scheme has been that the rates being paid were challenged by the service users to come in line with European directives. The result is that service users can offer competitive terms and conditions to their recruited staff, providing an example of how the collaboration between the line managers, the training and development team and the service users themselves resulted in creating best practice.

Conclusion

The aim of this chapter has been to explore the central role of the professional social work manager within the social care governance framework. Social work has already some of the structures in place to ensure governance. The line manager is critical in taking all the professional and organisational loose strands and creating congruence for social workers in understanding the mutual dependence of the PQ, organisational accreditation, standards and audit. The focus on clinical governance gave the impetus to develop an integrated framework with the result that the same work provides evidence for all of the above initiatives. We need to give credit for social work having instinctively gone in the right direction and to plan for the future by consciously and reflectively working to standards and audit agenda, strengthening the research base and publicly celebrating the many examples of excellent practice. Success breeds success.

References

Brearley, C.P. (1982) *Risk in Social Work*. London: Routledge and Kegan Paul.

DHSS (Department of Health and Social Services) (1998) *Community Care From Policy to Practice; the Case of Frederick Joseph McLernon (deceased)* London: NHS Executive, Belfast: DHSS.

DHSSPS (Department for Health, Social Services and Public Safety) (2001) *Best Practice, Best Care*. Belfast: DHSSPS.

DHSSPS (Department for Health, Social Services and Public Safety) (2002) *The Employer of Choice.*. Belfast: DHSSPS.

Egan, G. (1990) *The Skilled Helper: A Systematic Approach to Effective Helping*. (4th ed) Pacific Grove, California: Brooks-Cole Publishing Company.

Hawkins, P. and Shohet, R. (2000) *Supervision in the Helping Professions*. Buckingham: Open University Press.

Kadushin, A. (1976) 'Maps and Models of Supervision.' In P. Hawkins and R. Shonet (eds) (2000) *Supervision In the Helping Professions.* Buckingham: Open University Press.

McCullagh, M. (2001) Personal communication.

NHS (1998) *A First Class Service.* White Paper. London: Department of Health.

Pincus, A. and Minahan, A. (1973) *Social Work Practice: Model and Method.* Itasca, IL: F.E. Peacock.

Shulman, L. (1999) *The Skills of Helping Individuals, Families and Groups.* Itasca, IL: F.E. Peacock.

Smyth, C., Simmons, L. and Cunningham, G. (1999) *Quality Assurance in Social Work.* London: NISW.

Taylor, B. and Devine, T. (1993) *Assessing Need and Planning Care in Social Work.* Aldershot: Ashgate.

CHAPTER 6

First Line Managers

The Mediators of Standards and the Quality of Practice

Patricia Kearney

This chapter looks at the circumstances needed for good practice in social work and for social care to flourish. It looks in particular at the role and function of first line managers in promoting and sustaining practice standards, drawing on work undertaken by the National Institute for Social Work (NISW). It considers some of the relevant literature and the current state of research in this area. The chapter concludes with some thoughts about the proposed changes to social work training and how these could contribute to the management of practice.

Because first line managers go under various job titles within and across agencies, they are defined here as an individual, in any social care setting, with responsibility for managing the direct practice and service delivery of a group of staff.

'Managing practice' encompasses a range of first-line manager activities. These include individual supervision but also formal team supervision, to capture collective expertise and collaborative effort. Managing practice is what the manager does to combine available knowledge, external standards, statutory requirements and organisational procedures so that they form an integrated support to the individual and collective good practice and decision making of the team.

Over the last twenty years or so what social workers actually do has become an increasingly fragmented notion: social work and social care have been affected directly and indirectly in the changes required of public services by central governments, in particular local government. Successive administrations have been intent on centralising power and decision making away from town halls, demanding savings and 'efficiency' and applying untried and untested management models to the welfare sphere (for a helpful account see Pollitt 1993). Major social care legislation, in particular the Children Act 1989 and the NHS and Community Care Act 1991, has been introduced and implemented against this background. The unintended, if not entirely unpredictable, consequence has been confusion between managing practice, that is, the quality and effectiveness of direct work with service users and carers, and managing the organisation. The supportive organisational frameworks intended to clarify and support ease assessment; service provision and its development have taken precedence over the exercise of professional skill and decision making. Parry-Jones and Soulsby (2001) give a typical example.

> The social services resource panel may increase parity within each authority and take the burden of accountability off practitioners' shoulders, but appears to leave them with an administrative assessment function and a reduced sense of professional autonomy. (p.425)

At the same time, in another part of the wood, service users and carers have found their voices and expect to be major players in service standards and development. Paradoxically, this comes at a time when their disjointed work environment makes it difficult for social work and social care to respond to users' expectations.

The imbalance between systems and practice was noted in the review of the Diploma in Social Work training (JM Consulting 1999) commissioned by the Department of Health to inform its proposed changes to the qualification.

> Social workers could be seen as operating under supervision within a pre-determined framework of procedures and not required to exercise independent judgement (or) that social workers need...qualities of independent thought and critical analysis skills...not just to perform

competently in routine situations but to challenge, question and adapt their practice to the needs of particular clients and circumstances. This includes having the self-confidence to know when they are not able to perform safely and effectively and must seek help. (para 3.7–9)

More recently, the Victoria Climbié Inquiry has graphically demonstrated how front-line agencies lose sight of their practice functions and goals if they do not understand and implement the fundamental principles of practice, subsuming organisational maintenance to the service of risk assessment and decision making.

> It is also interesting that the Part 8 review, the thing I have actually read, whilst it painted an appalling picture of failure, mainly focuses on individual decisions, failure and the inability of agencies, multi-agencies to work together as opposed to systems which failed. I believe those systems are actually there. (Gurbux Singh, previously Chief Executive, Haringey Council, reported in Climbié Inquiry 2001a)

Good practice outcomes, unless specifically looked for, will be like dusting the parlour: only noticed by their absence. NISW's Management of Practice Expertise project examined the conditions that support good social care practice, and the implications for social work education and for expectations on employers.

The project asked what management approaches best enable staff to develop and sustain their practice expertise (Kearney 1999). Its findings concluded that first line managers hold a pivotal role as arbiters of practice standards, the 'keystone' of the organisation.

The team supervision and development material produced during the project (Rosen 1998) indicates the skills required of first-line managers. In summary, an effective team manager should be able to:

- manage practice, including supervision of individual and collective team practice, management of workloads, workflow, service development and the administrative and finance systems to support these

- offer supervision that takes into account the emotional impact of the work and its effect on individual and organisational working

- know about, understand and integrate required standards for practice within the team's work

- contribute to the professional development of team members, collectively and individually

- model and describe a professional approach to the work including appropriate use of authority, autonomy, responsibility and accountability, and expect and enable staff to understand and demonstrate this in their own work.

Finally, and importantly, the project's findings set out the relationship between managing practice and managing the organisation. The barriers, supports and systemic changes that emerge when first-line managers undertake this work are charted in Rosen (2000).

The project endorsed the particular role of first line managers in sustaining practice standards. In the project first line managers met together, often for the first time, to collaborate on and develop their role as educators and arbiters of practice standards. Organisations needed to create opportunities and expectations so that these groups worked together, pooling experience and knowledge, on practice and service development. It was clear that first line managers were most effective in developing practice standards when they worked with their teams collectively as well as supervising individual members. Finally the organisation received maximum benefit from this approach when it harnessed these efforts to inform and develop the whole organisation, making systemic change a continuous process.

When NISW overviewed the literature in this field in 1995 at the start of the project it found that it was mostly contained within the literature on social work supervision but that even this had diminished during the previous decade, with little attention paid to the day-to-day context of operational services or of the tensions and integrations within the wider organisational system. Seminal work such as that of Schon (1987), Menzies Lyth (1988) and Mattinson (1975) did not appear to have much influence on how social care agencies undertook their business during the 1980s to 1990s.

One of the reasons for a falling off in this area of practice theory was because, in Britain at least, the notion of supervision had fallen into disrepute. This was understandable where poor or untrained supervision practice often reduced supervision to a semi-private activity, focused more on the individual, their work and the organisation's needs than on the outcomes for service users. Without standards and accountability supervision, at its worst, allowed abuses of power.

The bridge between management and practice provided by supervision was lost. The lack of visibility and accountability made supervision vulnerable to managerialist approaches and it has often become procedurally driven. The consequence is that the relationship between practitioner and supervisor is therefore likely to be a prescriptive one, as managers oversee compliance with procedural and fiscal requirements. It appears common-place for supervision to be regarded as no longer a part of a manager's job. There is a sense of fragmentation, where managers and practitioners inhabit parallel worlds with no awareness of a common purpose. Supervision has become a lost art, newer first-line managers are not taught how to supervise and supervision's contribution to maintaining standards has been forgotten.

This is a major loss since some of the best characteristics of supervision are vital to managing practice. Disengagement and reflection are essential to good practice and outcomes that are user centred. Supervision allows time for both. It also gives an opportunity to question practice and custom, vital to the individual's practice development and ultimately to effective services. With the impact, intended and unforeseen, of general management approaches upon the public services throughout the past two decades, interest in alternative relationships between management and practice have begun to grow. More recent texts consider the organisational context within which social work and social care operated and had to be managed: Brown and Bourne (1996) comment on 'the agency–practice interface' (p.72); Riley (1997) considers the supervision received by social care managers.

There is little larger-scale research on supervision in social care and there is a clear need for this to inform the increasing initiatives and changes intended to support practice standards if the field is to be able to evaluate its efforts. The study by Marsh and Triseliotis (1996) is one such, examining workers' 'readiness to practice' one year after qualification. As part of this research, Marsh and Tresiliotis asked first-line managers about their expectations of newly qualified workers. Responses indicate that some managers consider that preparing and developing staff should happen 'at college', not at work, prompting the authors to ask, 'whose responsibility is it to help the newly qualified understand administration, paper work, guidelines and procedures – that of the course or induction?' (p.127). The study charts workers' experiences of supervision, good and bad, and highlights the difficulties that arise when organisations and managers do not integrate managing practice within their role:

> The general consensus, among both the newly qualified and seniors within the social work (services) departments, was that management has to recognise the centrality of the quality of supervision to the effectiveness of the work of the newly qualified and plan for it accordingly. (p.164)

Other recent literature shows a growing interest in putting together the individual and the collective, professional autonomy and organisational membership, and internal and external processes, that is, the task required of the first line manger, whether implicitly or explicitly, to manage practice and manage the organisation.

This has come from various directions. Froggett (2000) considers the organisational potential of supervision by analysing the process undertaken within a social services department to create and implement a supervision policy. She argues that a good supervision policy fosters 'a containing environment in which anxiety can be acknowledged, explored, shared and maintained within acceptable boundaries' (p.34). Morrison (2001) takes into account that the social care workforce is made up of a variety of staff, with a range of backgrounds and qualifications. First-line managers need to manage practice in its diverse forms. Morrison focuses on the day-to-day development work required by social care teams if they are to sustain effective practice. Presented as a training manual, his work combines theory and practice on developing standards so that the reality of daily work is always present. He demonstrates the breadth and level of skill required to manage direct practice. Turner (2000) looks at the role of mentors within the post-qualifying framework. Although her argument highlights the development needs of managers in the context of mentoring post-qualification education, this can equally be applied to the mainstream responsibility of managing practice. The barriers to mentoring that Turner reports have implications for managing practice, particularly the opinion voiced by one practitioner who would be 'more open to acknowledge weaknesses if the mentor wasn't the line manager' (p.236).

This split between 'good/powerless' and 'bad/powerful' advisors is demonstrated in the Climbié Inquiry (2001b):

> Mr Garnham (barrister): Did you understand in the summer of 1999 that social workers would need the authority of their managers to contact you?
>
> Ms Kitchman (child protection adviser): That was not my understanding, no.
>
> Mr Garnham: Do you mean by that that your understanding was the reverse, namely that they could contact you without the approval of their managers?
>
> Ms Kitchman: Yes.
>
> Mr Garnham: Were social workers entitled to reject your advice?
>
> Ms Kitchman: That is a difficult way of wording it. They were not entitled to reject our advice, no, but sometimes...
>
> Mr Garnham: Were they obliged to follow it?
>
> Ms Kitchman: They were obliged to follow it but that did not always happen...
>
> Mr Garnham: Lisa Arthurworrey (social worker)...understood that she could only use one of you on the recommendation or with the approval of a manager but you say that is not your understanding?
>
> Ms Kitchman: No, that is not my understanding.
>
> Mr Garnham: She also told Mr Monaghan that where contradictory advice was received from you on the one hand and her manager on the other she was obliged to do what her manager said. Was that your understanding?

> Ms Kitchman: No...I think it was not an option, but that nevertheless sometimes our advice was overruled by team managers and we would not always know about that.

Here the management of practice is seen as a matter of hierarchical systems when coping with conflicts rather than as seeing differences and disagreements of view as part of the resource for analysing and working with complex practice issues.

Some of the difficulties noted by Turner (2000) may be more readily solved if they are understood as showing the emotional impact of the work. This is not to be confused with the issue of 'staff care', which may seek to protect individuals from this kind of exposure. A practitioner's uncomfortable feelings, including being frightened, are a useful assessment tool and they need to remain open to such feelings. To help them do this safely and effectively a supervisor needs to be an anchor and a guide. Organisations are made up of individuals whose unacknowledged emotions will affect organisational as well as individual performance if there is no place for them to be acknowledged as a consequence of the work both staff and managers are doing.

Couper (2000) develops this theme within the context of working with sexually abused children. He describes some of the direct and indirect ways this impact manifests itself in individual and team performance and the organisation's responsibility for managing these processes so that they become informative rather than damaging. This strand of the literature tends to concentrate its examples within child protection services. However, it is common to all work in the helping professions where dealing with distress, loss and sometimes irreconcilable interests are the norm. I give a recent example of observed practice noted during NISW's preparation for a project on working with older people.

> A social worker undertaking initial assessments of older people at home was observed travelling back and forth to her office, some distance away, although her visits were often in adjoining streets. When asked why she didn't undertake some of the visits one after the other, the worker had to think, as she hadn't been aware of her behaviour. She was surprised at herself as she was always looking for more time to reflect on her work.

Eventually she said: 'You know, I think it's just that I can't bear it when I can't do much to help people who are in such distress.'

Feelings and thoughts move across the boundaries of professional and personal, individual and organisational in less than obvious ways. Organisations that know this and how to manage these processes give themselves a rich source for understanding positive practice change. Organisations that push them underground will struggle to do their job well.

Trowell and Miles (1991), in their account of the post-Cleveland training initiatives, show the impact of feelings on performance and its implications for training and development in the field of child protection. Hughes and Pengelly (1997) extend the scope of this approach and consider the effect on the wider organisation and the role of managers in understanding and dealing with this process.

Outside Britain there has continued to be an interest in supervision, its functions and techniques. This has been especially so in the USA, where the notion of 'clinical supervision' is current, for example, through publications such as *Clinical Social Work Journal*. In Australia, where social work practice and its structures have similar roots to British contingents, the recent literature has shown a growing interest in supervision and management. Examples include Clare (2001), Itzhaky and Ribner (1998), Itzhaky (2000) and Gibbs (2001).

Social work training has always had a strong practice emphasis with placements as a required element of qualifying courses. This continues in the new social work qualification with the assertion that social work is a 'practical activity'. That is, it is insufficient to know *about* practice, the requirement is to be able *to practice* to a set standard. Whilst this approach has had many unsatisfactory aspects, including difficulty in obtaining placements with employers and in ensuring standards of teaching and performance, the concept remains sound. It is likely that in the future development opportunities will need to be linked to current employment. 'Learning at work' is evolving beyond its sparsest definition as a workplace that encourages its staff to take up qualifications. The interplay between thinking and doing, about learning from the work you do and how you do it, is a complex one, and may not be a cheap or easy option for employers.

Pottage and Evans (1994) describe this kind of environment as a 'competent workplace'.

> The features of the competent or learning workplace involve a radical change in internal working patterns and relationships, affecting all activity. Our evidence supports the view that, to achieve meaningful innovation, development must arise from and be based on day-to-day experience – a reservoir of information and intelligence that normally remains hidden. The foundation for future professional competence is to develop the capacity of the individual (and the workplace) to learn how to learn. (p.6)

Increasingly, social care employers should expect to be involved in the professional education of their staff. The General Social Care Council (2001) code of practice for employers requires that they:

- regularly supervise and effectively manage staff to support good practice and professional development and to address any deficiencies in their performance

- provide training and development opportunities to help staff to do their jobs and to strengthen and develop their skills and knowledge

- contribute to the provision of social care and social work education and training, and provide properly resourced and managed workplace assessment and opportunities for practice learning.

Another influence has been the growth of 'evidence-based' and latterly, 'knowledge-based' approaches to practice and management. That is, enquiry as to the knowledge available from a range of sources and how it can be used to enhance the quality of social care. This approach is reflected, for example, in the National Service Frameworks where current best practice, including professional consensus, is charted. Resources such as Research in Practice http://www.rip.org.uk/ and Making Research Count http://www.uea.ac.uk/swk/research/mrc/welcome.htm are now available to the social care field. The Social Care Institute for Excellence (SCIE) http://www.scie.org.uk has been set up with a remit to 'collate, translate and disseminate' knowledge in social care. It houses the Electronic Library in Social Care (eLSC). SCIE maintains the social care database, reSearchWeb http://www.researchweb.org.uk/ for the Scottish Executive.

The last two years have seen major developments in the social care field that offer positive change. They include central government support for a robust and sufficient workforce, begun in 2002 with the Department of Health advertising campaign; the creation of formal standards and registration requirements, and the development of a new social work qualification at degree level. All of these developments show the emerging expectation that practitioners will develop critical autonomy in their work and take professional responsibility for their decisions. Managers will be expected to manage these staff appropriately and assist them in developing these capabilities. An example of this aspect of the manager's work is the material published by TOPSS (2001) on how managers can use occupational standards with their staff as part of their professional development.

The conditions in place to support the development and maintenance of these first-line managers include:

- published standards for first-line managers, including a 'ready to practice' standard to parallel that of the DipSW, and for these to be reflected in the new PQ frameworks

- an expectation/requirement of employers to have an appropriate supervision policy and implementation process in place

- an expectation/requirement of employers to ensure that first-line managers have supervision skills. The current Practice Teachers Award, which is often seen by workers and organisations as an alternative to progression to team manager, could provide a basis for this. This work could begin at senior practitioner level as a preparation for management

- an expectation/requirement of employers to ensure first-line managers have management of practice skills and the provision of appropriate training in managing practice for first-line managers, following on from supervision training, as part of the organisation's management development strategy.

Robust practice will be aided by a number of factors, including appropriately trained practitioners appropriately managed, equally prepared first-line managers, social care agencies that value the management of practice and national requirements that encourage and sustain these approaches. Future arrangements for management development, post-qualifying training and organisational development should reflect the potential of first-line managers as standard setters and educators.

References

Brown, A. and Bourne, I. (1996) *The Social Work Supervisor: Supervision in Community, Day Care and Residential Settings.* Buckingham: Open University Press.

Clare, M. (2001) 'Operationalising Professional Supervision in this Age of Accountabilities.' *Australian Social Work 54*, 2, 69–79.

Climbié Inquiry (2001a) 'The Victoria Climbié Inquiry.' Archived transcript for 18 December. http://www.victoria-climbie-inquiry.org.uk/index.htm

Climbié Inquiry (2001b) 'The Victoria Climbié Inquiry.' Archived transcript for 10 December. http://www.victoria-climbie-inquiry.org.uk/index.htm

Couper, D. (2000) 'The Impact of the Sexually Abused Child's Pain on the Worker and the Team.' *Journal of Social Work Practice 14*,1, 9–16.

Froggett, L. (2000) 'Staff Supervision and Dependency Culture: A case study.' *Journal of Social Work Practice 14*, 1, 27–35.

Gibbs, J.A. (2001) 'Maintaining Front-line workers in Child Protection: A case for refocusing supervision.' *Child Abuse Review 10*, 5, 323–335.

General Social Care Oouncil (2001) http://www.codes-consultation.co.uk/english /text2.html

Hughes, L. and Pengelly, P. (1997) *Staff Supervision in a Turbulent Environment: Managing Process and Task in Front-line Services.* London: Jessica Kingsley.

Itzhaky, H. (2000) 'The Secret in Supervision: An integral part of the social worker's professional development.' *Families in Society: The Journal of Contemporary Human Services 71*, 5, 529–537.

Itzhaky, H. and Ribner, D.S. (1998) 'Resistance as a Phenomenon in Clinical and Student Social Work Supervision.' *Australian Social Work 51*, 3, 25–29.

JM Consulting (1999) *Review of the Diploma in Social Work: Report on the content of the DipSW conducted as part of the Stage Two Review of CCETSW.* Report to the Department of Health.

Kearney, P. (ed) (1999) *Managing Practice: Report on the Management of Practice Expertise Project.* London: National Institute for Social Work.

Marsh, P. and Triseliotis, J. (1996) *Readiness to Practise: The Training of Social Workers in Scotland and their First Year in Work.* Edinburgh: Scottish Office Central Research Unit.

Mattinson, J. (1975) *The Reflection Process in Casework Supervision.* London: Institute of Marital Studies, Tavistock Institute of Human Relations.

Menzies Lyth, I. (1988) 'The Functioning Of Social Defence Systems as a Defence Against Anxiety.' In *Containing Anxiety in Institutions: Selected essays; Volume 1.* London: Free Association Books.

Morrison, T. (2001) *Staff Supervision in Social Care,* 2nd ed. Brighton: Pavilion.

Parry-Jones, B. and Soulsby, J. (2001) 'Needs-led Assessment: The challenges and the reality.' *Health and Social Care in the Community 9,* 6, 414–28.

Pollitt, C. (1993) *Managerialism and the Public Services.* Oxford: Blackwell.

Pottage, D. and Evans, M. (1994) *The Competent Workplace: The View From Within.* London: National Institute for Social Work.

Riley, P. (1997) 'Supervision of Social Service Managers.' In J. Pritchard (ed) *Good Practice in Supervision: Statutory and Voluntary Agencies.* London: Jessica Kingsley Publishers.

Rosen, G. (ed) (1998) *Managing Team Development: A Short Guide for Teams and Team Managers.* London: National Institute for Social Work.

Rosen, G. (ed) (2000) *Integrity, the Organisation and the First-line Manager: Discussion papers.* London: National Institute for Social Work.

Schon, D. A. (1987) *Educating the Reflective Practitioner: Toward a New Design for Teaching and Learning in the Professions.* San Francisco: Jossey-Bass.

TOPSS (2001) 'Manager's Guide to Developing Strategic Uses of National Occupational Standards.' http://www.topss.org.uk/pdf/man_guide_strat_NOS.pdf

Trowell, J. and Miles, G. (1991) 'The Contribution of Observation Training to Professional Development in Social Work.' *Journal of Social Work Practice 5,* 1, 51–60.

Turner, B. (2000) 'Supervision and Mentoring in Child and Family Social Work: The role of the first-line manager in the implementation of the post -qualifying framework.' *Social Work Education 19,* 3, 231–240.

CHAPTER 7

Managing Duty Teams in Children's Services

Eva Learner and Gwen Rosen

> It is important also that each social service department has a structure and systems in place to ensure effective, accessible and speedy responses to children and families.
>
> (Assessment Framework 2001)

Introduction

Duty or assessment and referrals teams are the doorway to the services. The first contact sets the tone for future relationships. The duty team is not simply the gateway to services for children and families or for preventing serious harm, vital though that is. Duty teams influence children's life chances by opening up access to services that can promote their health, education and well-being.

The complex interaction between a child's physical environment, the family economy and their life chances is the reason that the *Framework for the Assessment of Children in Need* was jointly produced by the Department of Health, the Department of Education and Skills, and the Home Office (2001). Although this partnership is new, the content of the Assessment Framework is not. The Assessment Framework scheme reflects good child care practice and has become a national requirement and a useful practice tool. It is available not only to social workers and their managers but also to parents, young people and their advocates. This is new and has major implications for practice.

It was against this policy context that we undertook work with teams located mainly in disadvantaged areas in Central London as well as with some in Outer London and in other parts of England and Wales. In the process, more fully described in Learner and Rosen (2001), we were outsiders but not consultants in the traditional sense of the word. We were brought in to encourage change by developing practice skills in good management and group processes. The work was often with teams overwhelmed by complex problems and long waiting lists. In places some children were endangered because of poorly organised services. All boroughs reported recruitment and retention problems and high sick leave as well as a history of unsuccessful attempts to improve operations. In some cases the Social Service Inspectorate had found practice standards wanting with unhelpful, redundant administrative systems and a lack of control of the work. Often the workflow and team arrangements had been weakened by a wave of departmental restructuring, along with poor systems for managing front line practice and the shortage of social workers. The response to referrals had either been too slow or not forthcoming, and the confidence of professional colleagues in health and education had been undermined.

Duty teams deal with problems that are likely to be of a deeply personal and intimate kind. They frequently involve family relationships, complex behaviour and working with people who use services reluctantly. However, many problems can be resolved simply by offering opportunities for support such as welfare rights or housing advice, or through community-based services such as Sure Start and family centres. Not all duty work is highly complex.

Creating Change in Duty Teams

The approach we used for initiating and managing change applies broadly to all teams and groups. Knowledge of the following three areas is essential:

- the management of practice
- the processes of developing groups

- knowledge of good social work practice.

Together these enabled us to take a holistic approach to managing change in duty teams. The added dimension in our work is that we, as the change agents, were brought in from outside the local authority with firm links to the National Institute for Social Work (NISW) whose mission was to promote excellence in practice. We had explicit agreements with senior managers in the commissioning social service departments that we would take a hands-on approach at all levels of management and with team members. These agreements were reviewed at regular intervals with all involved so that there was transparency about what our contribution was and any conflicts or confusions were resolved rapidly. This process models the patterns of communication we were trying to develop – communication about what needed to change, its time scales and how it would be achieved. The change agents consulted and worked alongside staff at the front line as well as with front-line managers and senior management. It was essential that we demonstrated that we were trustworthy and open in the way we worked. The two change agents worked in tandem. One change agent had primary responsibility for working at the front line while the other provided back-up and attended meetings with senior managers to discuss progress and planning.

The change agent's role

Change is the one constant in all organisations, and managing change is intrinsic to the pursuit of excellence. Change can be about very minor matters or major structural reorganisation. It is essential to know which of these orders of change is being attempted because the management task is different in each case. Minor changes are incremental and do not require radical shifts in hearts, minds and practices. Major change requires negotiation and processes that are transparent at all levels in the organisation. There must be clear accountability for managing the process of change and for decisions taken as a result.

Managing the change process needs to be the specific responsibility of a particular person or group, although managers at all levels are to some extent change agents in organisations (Kanter, Stein and Jick 1992). Managers routinely undertake the initiation and development of change in the teams for which they are responsible. It is perfectly possible for managers to undertake most of the work we describe, and often a task force will be set up comprising people with the appropriate expertise from the organisation. However, there are times when it is appropriate to bring people with specific expertise into the organisation as the change may require specialist expertise and independence. This combination can be powerful when internal efforts to achieve change have been ineffective. The external person(s) can be more persuasive to a sceptical and demoralised team and bring a new perspective to what may seem to be a 'stuck' situation. Staff may carry with them much of the history and the myths associated with team problems of which they have been a part, although often unwillingly or unwittingly.

In our work the teams gave us a number of reasons why they were unconvinced about any changes actually happening. Examples included that they:

- had suggested particular changes over many months but were never heard by their managers
- were not respected by senior management
- had to work in cramped and poor working conditions
- were enormously overstretched, and management did not believe what they said
- had spent time planning and preparing, and the goal posts had changed
- found agreements were never followed through.

Usually the teams had a history of being restructured; members were angry and the team itself operated in a fragmented way and provided little support for members. They were resistant to change because there was a culture that 'the way we did things in the old days was best'. This is reminiscent of Marsh and Fisher's (1992) work where they found in a number of organisations that a powerful determinant of practice was 'the way it is done here'. There tended to be an unusually large number of staff on sick leave and the teams were generally pessimistic about any change being implemented in a systematic way. In these organisations we found that managers had tried hard to introduce order in working practice and team development but were losing heart, increasingly were unable to operate effectively as managers and were beginning themselves to identify with the positions adopted by the team members.

In these circumstances an external change agent can be a useful method of promoting change. Senior managers and, in a number of cases external inspection, had clearly identified what the problems were and had agreed what needed to change to raise standards. Trust was established through concentrating initially on simple pragmatic problems that were easily solved. These were often the areas that had been identified by the managers and the team as those that had failed to attract the attention of senior management. Achieving even minuscule change rapidly was sufficient to allow us to agree a working mode with the teams and for them to have a sense of empowerment because they had already identified these as issues before we arrived. This is consistent with management theory that recommends 'trying out small changes before developing formalised strategies, as they allow for trying out alternatives without posing great risks, promoting professional growth' (Kanter, Stein and Jick 1992).

The front door

Speed and efficiency of response to the problems brought to the duty teams are critical. At initial contact the nature of the request for assistance may not always be clear. Correct and full basic information will save time later and supports a more accurate diagnosis of need. The Assessment Framework requirements begin to operate immediately and reception staff, whether part of the formal intake team or not, are part of the process. The duty manager's task must include working with the administrative staff and their supervisors to integrate their reception work with the natural flow of the intake system. Hall (1974), Burchell (1992) and more recently the National Task Force on Violence Towards Social Care Staff (2001) all emphasise the importance of reception staff receiving support and training for a demanding job. As the first point of contact this will influence attitudes to individual staff members as well as to the department. It can also influence the quality of subsequent communications and future co-operation. A response by reception staff reflecting an open, friendly and professional demeanour, whether by phone or at the desk, is likely to elicit more information and a clearer picture of the matter of concern than impatient, off-hand, irritable or angry responses. Information from receptionists should always be a part of the resource to the duty team and they give advice and information to service users as part of their gatekeeping and screening role.

Accountability of administrative staff

A good service is the synthesis of its various parts, and administrative support is intrinsic to a professional service. We found that accountability of the administrative staff, whether at reception or providing support to the duty team, was a serious problem in organisations where SSI reported that practice had fallen to unacceptable levels. The commitment and loyalty of the administrative staff to the duty team was crucial whatever structure was used. Problems were worse where there was confusion about accountability, whether to their direct supervisor or to the duty manager. The degree to which administrative supervisors intervened in the day-to-day work varied. This was not found to be related either to the number of the staff involved or to the demands of the workload. Sometimes the administrative supervisor followed the duty administrative assistants closely, almost directing their tasks throughout the day; in other places they played a more traditional role, supervising staff on a regular basis and expecting them to be directed by and accountable to the duty team manager for their day-to-day work. In the latter model the administrative supervisor was only called in when there was a problem or to clear confusion about a procedure.

In general, we found the latter model worked best. Irrespective of the managerial solution a great deal of work was necessary to facilitate coherence between the different staff's contributions to making a duty team effective. Administrative staff, including their supervisors and senior managers, must understand the context of the duty team's work and the vital contribution the administrative staff make to that work.

In all the duty teams we worked with development sessions were held with administrative supervisory staff, along with duty administrative assistants to clarify confusion, boundaries, tasks and roles. There were also sessions with the whole duty team where both the administrative supervisor and the duty team manager gave presentations about how they each contributed to good and safe practice. This set up a new relationship between different groups of staff and began to free up the administrative staff to commit themselves to the work of the duty team. Four- to six-weekly meetings between the administrative staff and the duty manager(s) ensured that this collaboration continued and provided a forum to discuss current issues and problems and better ways to manage the administrative work.

The duty team skill mix

The traditional approach to duty teams in children's services is that they are staffed by qualified social workers. Recently a different model of the staffing and structure of the duty team has begun to emerge, with staff from different backgrounds being employed in these teams. There remains a debate about whether to continue to use only the most skilled workers or whether well trained non social work staff can undertake this very responsible task as well.

Where the duty team has staff with a mix of skills and non social work backgrounds these staff are being used in two main ways. In some places, the intake duty desk may be staffed by non social work staff, often administrative officers, and/or reception staff. The central role for this group of staff is to process only the initial request for assistance. They may complete an initial referral form and then pass the request to the social work team who undertake the initial assessment. They also perform a very important advice and information task, mostly focused on welfare rights, housing, and general information about health or education services.

Within the rest of the team of social workers there may be graduates with nursing qualifications or human science graduates with sociology and anthropology degrees. These people are employed as family support workers or welfare workers. They will assist social workers and/or undertake appropriate assessments of requests for financial or other matters.

Our experience has been with intake duty teams that have used administrative staff only at the reception or intake desk and also with teams that have used a mix of social work and administrative officers to undertake the intake process. Providing the non social work group of staff is adequately trained and closely monitored, supported and supervised, and has easy access to the duty manager or senior practitioners, they can offer a helpful and safe service.

We found that intake team members wanted and needed to work closely with the duty manager and the social work teams. They were usually confident and open about approaching the manager and other team staff for guidance. More of a problem was the scale of induction and training they required. We found, for example, that special topics relating to the information and advice knowledge base need to be repeated annually, and new material added. The intake team also had meetings with key staff in other organisations with whom it worked closely, such as housing and community ethnic groups, as a means of increasing understanding about working together. A good community resource library and index system was set up as part of our work. The whole duty team, therefore, has ready access to lists of all local schools, health centres, voluntary organisations, publications of community-based organisations and information about charities. However, until the model using nontrained social workers in duty intake is formally evaluated and researched it cannot be said with certainty whether this model is to be preferred over the more traditional one.

The use of nonqualified workers is not new. Historically support staff not trained in social work have been used in the casework teams working with children in a number of fields. Known also as family support workers, they have undertaken a number of practical tasks to assist the social worker. Welfare rights workers are another group providing a critical service in a number of agencies. The mental health field pioneered non social work-qualified workers in day-to-day support in the community and increasingly former service users are assisting in a professional capacity in user-controlled and community-based organisations. Current policy both values multidisciplinary teams and the expertise and experience of people who use services as a resource in practice and service development (Department of Health 2000).

The present severe shortage of both social work and social care staff is likely to persist for some time. The length of time it takes to train a social worker is one factor. Demographic trends mean that there is greater competition for the fewer young people coming on to the labour market, and women, by far the largest proportion of the social care workforce (Balloch, McLean and Fisher 1999), have a wider range of employment options than in the past. These combined trends mean that serious consideration needs to be given to using non-social work qualified staff as members of intake teams. Although training, systematic supervision and monitoring is required, this model of intake team is a valid option of coping with a difficult labour market. It is essential that a change to mixed skill duty teams is planned and managed and is not a haphazard development.

Social work practice in duty teams

Current social work practice on the front line is being shaped, more than is probably recognised, by the Assessment Framework introduced by the Department of Health. The Children Act 1989, emphasised the need for speedy responses to new referrals, but social services inspection reports over the years showed this was not happening.

The Assessment Framework

In the social services departments where the two authors worked it took some two years to achieve recognisable and sustained change in the quality of practice. Changes in practice take time to implement if they are to be sustained. The Assessment Framework was used as a support to practice and a tool rather than a 'tick box' approach that undermines professional judgement and expertise. The Assessment Framework also marks a change in culture for many organisations. It recommends time-scales for specific assessments and methods for monitoring these in ways that have not been previously experienced by managers. Achieving targets, such as completing the initial assessment in seven working days, has been a challenge for many teams because firm time-spans are often seen as difficult to manage for front-line workers.

Social workers in all aspects of children and family work are expected to have basic social work skills, but the routine need for speed of response in duty teams makes it unlike work in children in need or looked after children's teams. There is little time for workers in duty teams to be nurtured in the slower supportive way that is possible in other teams. The bombardment, complexity and challenge excite a particular mix of heightened activity, fast-pace working that can be addictive if the worker enjoys this style of work but can be very stressful to others. The manager and the workers must be aware of this and be able to develop approaches to manage this context. The work requires good assessment skills, a solid knowledge base and a capacity to work with community-based organisations, especially those that form part of the Area Child Protection Committee (ACPC) network. Duty work also requires skills in crisis intervention because short-term work is the characteristic of the task. Workers in these teams need to be able to make appropriate assessments, and on occasion offer a brief service but then be able to withdraw and transfer the case effectively.

This mix of skills and the capacity to manage them are required for teams to respond efficiently and effectively within time-scales and often in high-risk situations for both children and their families. The process incorporates accurate diagnosis, analysis and the making of service recommendations. Evidence-based practice is also an aspect encouraged by the Assessment Framework that provides a whole series of well-articulated and accessible documents to assist workers in more accurate analyses based on research findings. In general we have found that social workers are often more focused on the descriptive elements of the assessment and fail to give sufficient attention to analysis and professional judgement that is backed up by research evidence.

The development of skills in practice

Where the teams we worked with had been assessed as performing below acceptable standards, raising standards was one part of the task, as was embedding continuing professional development as part of the culture of the whole team. Work with the whole team is essential. In all the teams there was a mix of agency and permanent staff, with a somewhat unpredictable turnover.

Systems development and circular processes

The work with teams required two main elements. The first was recognition that the process of change is difficult even when the current system is working. The second was that development in the quality of the practice could only be achieved by setting up systems that ensure transparent, efficient and effective processing of the work.

Systems underpin good practice in all teams, particularly where there is a sense of bombardment and a changing membership. Workflow systems must be identified, articulated and learned, along with the appropriate registration of the details of the enquiries and referrals on computer and manual systems. All workers must learn and understand the systems, their tasks and the contribution they make to duty work. We identified two different approaches used by managers to introduce new systems. One was gradual and the other was total radical change. In both cases we ensured that these changes were discussed and their introduction planned.

One of the most common problems in intake teams was the 'circular' movement of cases that were processed by different social workers during their rostered period on the duty desk. This could result in a number of social workers completing one assessment. The work in these instances tended to be of poor quality and the case could drift on the duty desk for days. Often the service user was unclear about progress or the identity of the social worker responsible.

We found that this confusion disadvantaged the service user in several ways and militated against good practice. If several social workers are involved in an assessment they are likely to duplicate effort because each worker may need to relearn the situation when they next pick up the case. Issues can become confused and the worker is more likely to 'fail' because of a lack of follow-up. Accountability is blurred and the worker–service user relationship will be complicated, particularly if users relate to more than one worker when they are experiencing difficulty and distress.

It was sometimes difficult to help teams to accept the principle of one worker completing an assessment when they had become used to this circular pattern. We used individual and group discussions but found that to embed the change often required a reconstitution of the team and new systems arrangements. Where there was major resistance a trial project was conducted with staff who were willing to take part. When they became convinced of the benefits of this approach it was more easily extended to the whole team. The changes introduced made the workflow feel safer and under greater control.

As change agents our role had to be eclectic in the sense of being able to use different approaches and skills as situations changed. We had to see the development of the duty team both as a whole and also as part of the total children and families service. We had to steer clear of any conflict between management and remain neutral in respect of internal politics. Where any guidance could be given, for example regarding a need for increased (or decreased) staffing resources, we would make recommendations. Similarly we had to handle situations when approaches recommended by other external advisors/consultants might be in conflict with our own perspective. If the department has commissioned other consultants, it is important to obtain permission from senior managers to meet and work together with them. Reasoned recommendations can then be made and there can be negotiations about what might be acceptable to all levels of management. Such ways of working enabled a control on the quality of our work, and with regular updating managers were aware of daily implementation. A senior manager, for example, was seen almost weekly, even just for a few moments. Managers were usually open and receptive to discussing the advice and recommendations made by the authors. It took time to establish trust with some managers, but this is vital and an integral part of any organisational change.

Management on Duty

What we found

Order is basic to good management in duty teams whether their location is a quiet rural area or a busy London authority. Whatever the model used for the intake team the workflow requires some form of systematic processing because most referrals are presented as urgent.

In the very busy inner-city areas we worked in the chaos which came in part from heavy referral rates and service demands and in part from a lack of systematic recording arrangements for allocating work. Staff felt overwhelmed, morale was low, and the managers did not feel in control of the workload. Often both workers and managers were fearful of the risk to children because they did not know exactly what was in the pile of case files lying on their desk.

The following list offers a useful check for managers and workers on the state and effectiveness of the duty team.

- Is there a large backlog of work, much of which rightly belongs in long-term teams and includes looked after children and complex children in need work?

- Is work difficult to pass from the duty team to the relevant teams because of a lack of staff in the long-term team or because there are tensions about what is appropriate to pass on and to whom? The longer the duty team continues to work with families, the harder it seems to let go of them. This backlog makes it difficult to sustain the regular processing of new referrals.

- Does administrative work reflect practice chaos such as

    - records showing an unrealistically high number of cases for the team

    - inaccurate records about whether cases are 'open' or 'closed'

    - case papers and files being lost while 'open to duty'

    - case papers and files lost in the archives?

Such inaccuracies in recording affect not only the day-to-day management of work with families but also the organisation's management information systems.

Management information

Management information other than the required national statistics appears not well integrated into the front line manager's day-to-day work. Lack of accurate recording and chaotic arrangements will affect the capacity of the manager to obtain sound management information that can be used to plan the work of the team and contribute strategically to the organisation as a whole. This role of the front line manager as a source of information is essential for both the team and strategic planning is only recently becoming understood by managers. Where accurate management information is used in daily work it is a good indicator of the efficiency of team practice and the level of the front line manager's expertise.

Supervision

The requirement on the duty desk for a speedy workflow, with accurate decision making and assessments that attend to eligibility, gatekeeping and screening, gives the duty team work its unique features. The manager must frequently help the worker to determine these decisions in the light of departmental protocols. Rapid decisions may have to be made by the manager on the next steps in the flow of the work and whether or not an initial assessment is required. This process necessitates a supervisory approach unusual in social work teams because managers should be actively involved on the front line, ensuring that decisions are right and that work is being processed. They must be at the desk, available and accessible for constant consultation. This supplements, but does not replace, the need for traditional regular supervision that considers the overall workload and provides professional support in practice and staff development. A criterion of the efficiency and effectiveness of the duty service is the quality of the supervision both on and off the duty desk.

Establishing Trust and Building Credibility

Establishing trust between the change agents and the team was our first step. In doing this we had also to demonstrate that we were credible and had expertise in child care and child protection and could cope with the chaos that was their day-to-day experience. Initially introductions and discussions were held with relevant managers at all levels. This led on to work with team managers on how to plan the steps to be taken and was followed by team meetings at which the broad objectives of our work were discussed. We also made a practice of chatting informally with members of the team. This had two purposes. The first was to provide information and to counter false rumours about what was happening. The second was to get information from them about their perceptions of problems and any solutions they might suggest.

The most powerful aspect of this approach was the opportunity it provided to work directly alongside team members in an informal way. We took whatever opportunity offered itself in a very natural way to assist team members with their practice and duty team work. In addition to answering the phone and helping to process referrals, we helped the duty desk when there was a shortage of staff. These activities took only a little of our time but made a significant contribution to helping staff become confident that we were there to learn and assist as well as introduce change. At the same time we demonstrated our capacity to understand and to know how to do the work involved. This way of working is one of the most rapid for learning the nature of the team's difficulties as well as modelling professional behaviour and standards of practice.

Achieving change is a process

The way in which we operated as external change agents involved demystifying the change process and working alongside the team rather than the more common consultancy approach that tends to direct from above or from outside and which most of the teams had experienced in the past. At the same time we were careful to have a clear action plan and time-frame. We also took care to distinguish our contribution from that of managers and to ensure that the managers' functions were enhanced rather than undermined in any way. The method we used to achieve this included regular reporting and discussions with team and senior management. It was essential to demonstrate that they held primary accountability for the work and at the same time we demonstrated that we had support from them. Kanter *et al.* (1992) recommend 'seeking support from power sources as well as stakeholders. Staff are intuitively aware of the importance of eliciting support from power sources'.

Ways of demonstrating our commitment to supporting the team in achieving changes included:

- answering the phone
- acting as an escort
- helping the team manager assess the backlog of work

- sharing information about the 'national picture'

- helping the manager to process backlogs of work

- walking the floor

- consulting the team

- being open to any discussion of practice issues that they wanted to raise with us.

Much of this seems very simple, but through it, we learned about the detail of the work and the problems that had to be dealt with for improvements in practice to take place. An example was the number of irrelevant or misdirected phone calls that are a frequent occurrence in duty teams. They can be easily diverted if the switchboard manager is aware of this problem and given a list of correct and up-to-date telephone numbers. Switchboard operators have a critical function in the referral system but they need to be kept informed.

The implications of change in the duty team

Change, even when it is contained and planned, will have widespread implications affecting other parts of the internal organisation and external organisations. Identifying who might be affected by the planned outcomes and how this will be handled is part of the management task, as is responding well to unexpected impacts or unintended outcomes. For example, the time-frame in the Assessment Framework scheme has had a distinct impact on the long term-teams in a number of local authorities since duty teams can no longer hold on to cases that require longer-term work. In some places this creates enormous pressures because many children with the status of looked after children have been held for various reasons in duty teams but are now being transferred. It is essential that any change planned in duty work is planned in unison with other teams working with children and families. The implications need to be identified and arrangements put in place to cope with them. Formal transfer meetings need to be established in order to help reduce the tensions between the receiving team and the duty team. If they persist, they reduce the safety of the service.

Similar planning has to take place to anticipate the impact of change on external organisations. For example, referrals to the duty team often have to be put on an external referral form. All organisations in the community need to be informed that verbal telephone referrals cannot be accepted other than in an emergency, and it follows that supplies of the referral forms must be available if the system is to work. In addition the required quality of information must be made clear and a way found to ensure that workers in these organisations understand why this is necessary for the safety of children and families and that it is not just as another bureaucratic imposition. As part of our change agent role we undertook this work and attended the Area Child Protection Committee meetings to follow up a letter describing the new system of duty.

Gathering information

Once the broad problems have been identified, the next step is to collect information and to identify what is actually happening and works well so that it can be given recognition and integrated into any new arrangements.

> A two pronged approach is recommended to get started. First concrete information about the realities of customers and employees needs to be collected. In this way, everyone can understand how 'the business actually works'. Secondly customers' and employees' hopes and dreams need to be reviewed. (Kanter *et al.* 1992)

Members at all levels of the department were asked to participate and time was spent thinking about better ways of serving children and their families through informal communication, education and training activities, and formal brainstorming sessions. For receptionists this included reviewing how they talked to people on the telephone; for front line workers it meant thinking about the many service users to be served; and for managers how the department could be organised in a way that would allow each person to perform his or her task optimally.

Current systems were observed in action – the workflow system; the backlog of cases awaiting management decisions and those still held by duty staff; the accuracy of recording systems, manual as well as computerised.

We analysed the information we had collected and checked our findings at team meetings specially arranged for this purpose. We wrote reports that identified what we saw as the state of the team's working arrangements and areas of concern. While transparency and openness is preferred these reports were written from a strategic point of view because this information is not always easily received and can exacerbate demoralisation. The change agents have to assess when the team has reached a stage where it is able to accept and believe that change is possible. As part of reaching this point there were regular feedback sessions held with the senior management staff about findings and suggested solutions. Senior managers attended some team meetings for discussions. As familiarity with the team and its way of working progressed, possible designs for solutions began to emerge from discussions. It was important that we were able to put the problems they were experiencing in a wider context and to tell the team when their problems were common to similar teams around the country. From this combination of resources we were able to build on the best of what existed.

Transforming to the new

Changes were often needed in the design of the workflow and the timing and nature of the administrative and management processes. We set these proposals out in diagrammatic form as well as in reports.

Agreement was sought from all staff in the duty team. Senior managers were well informed throughout about progress and issues. They undertook key strategic discussions, visited the team, and cleared any issues with other key individuals in the organisation and external agencies including the Area Child Protection Committee (ACPC).

We also provided a training programme for unqualified staff and development programmes for all staff selected for the intake task. The initial induction took place over four to five days and gave a basic introduction to the function and tasks of the team and the context of children and family work for example:

- the Children Act 1989, principles and regulations, including legal orders
- the Assessment Framework

- the context of child protection

- values and attitudes

- communication skills

- eligibility criteria, departmental protocols

- gatekeeping and screening

- the completion of the initial referral form

- housing legislation, social security benefits

- work with asylum seekers and with people who have overstayed their time in the UK

- Area Child Protection committees and the organisations they work with (for example schools, health and the police)

- working with difficult and violent service users.

Once agreement had been reached we planned very carefully a series of events about the action plan and its implementation. Significant among these were fixing the date when the new arrangements would begin and an 'away day' that we called the 'tuning in' day. The whole team – administrative staff, social workers, intake workers and team managers – was involved. The day introduced the new design of the team, work arrangements and their implications for practice, and how the Assessment Framework fitted into the new approach. This started a range of activities that addressed various aspects of the change plan. These included:

- reinforcement sessions which went over ground already covered so that it could be discussed in greater detail as the implementation of the plans began

- education and training sessions on specific areas of practice and on departmental policies and practice relating to thresholds.

With hindsight we should have consulted people using services about areas for improvement much earlier in the process. This could have been done through informal discussion in the waiting area, using the notice-board or more widely by advertising in the local press. Information about the new system needs to be provided for people using services and this could be in the form of a pamphlet. However, this is no substitute for staff knowing and being able to explain the system in person.

No effective change takes place overnight. It takes time to process the changes and for staff to move to a different mental framework in which they work efficiently but thoroughly on an initial assessment. Staff in the duty teams are currently in the next stage which is to develop their expertise in analysis and making recommendations about a service plan. The new systems will need to be kept under review as any new arrangements produce unforeseen problems. No system is set in stone and managers and the team must be able to identify what works well and what needs further change. Continued review of the team's performance, carried out by the team members, needs to be an ongoing process.

Consolidating, sustaining the new and moving on

Teams need to remain open to ongoing improvement and to accept that excellence is a journey and not a destination. A number of outcomes can be used as a measure of the degree of success and the changes instituted. These can include the following.

- The overall quality of the administrative and office systems will demonstrably indicate changes towards ordered systems. The previous chaotic approach will be visibly greatly reduced.

- Case files and papers will be accessible until there may be very few or none lost.

- The processes for tracking files and papers should be much clearer and concrete; for example, there will be either manual and/or computer systems available to indicate the whereabouts of the file or papers.

- Management information will be available in the form of simple but accurate statistics. These may be about the number and nature of enquiries per month, the number and nature of new referrals, and of listings of cases currently open to the duty team and the worker responsible.

- Regular supervision and support for the workers should be expected and should actually take place.

- Quality practice and learning on the job are complex matters. The availability of so many publications in the field of new research and evidence-based practice and the Assessment Framework scheme seem to have been a catalyst to on-the-job learning for workers. One of the changes that should be anticipated is a gradual but visible improvement in the quality of assessment work and report writing. Initial responses have caused some concern because workers sometimes perceive the reports as being an exercise in the 'tick-box' approach. But once workers are helped to use the Assessment Framework materials appropriately as a tool, then they can then undertake the assessments and reports required and the quality of their work should improve.

- We found that work in the duty teams often varied in the speed of work on assessments and the period of time a case remained in the team. The principle of a speedy response and the time-scales set by the Assessment Framework scheme has created a distinct change in the approach to time management of the work on duty. This is measurable, and can be used to help workers assess their own progress, at the same time recognising that assessments must not simply be directed by time-scale criteria.

- Changes should increase the feeling of empowerment of the team and its members. This is reflected in their demeanour and in workplace arrangements and environment. The workplace should feel much calmer than previously.

Other indicators of successful and observable change in the duty team include more enthusiasm for the work, more co-operative team relationships and a capacity and willingness to learn. In our work this was often reflected in greater participation in sharing ideas, offers to take on additional responsibilities, assisting one another with complex cases and the need to work extra hours. Team meetings may begin to be used in a very positive way rather than just being 'moaning sessions'. Reduced sick leave is a clear and visible indicator of positive change.

One of the most satisfying aspects of evidence for the changes is often in the behaviour of duty managers themselves. They develop a sense of empowerment and enthusiasm. They begin to devote some of their time to thinking about other work such as business plans or other strategic and corporate interests. Above all, and very rapidly, they may begin to articulate their feelings of being in control of the workflow and their belief that the service is now safe.

In our experience once the changes were established we as change agents were able to withdraw, at first gradually and then completely. It was necessary to remain involved for some time to consolidate the changes. We made four to five visits to the teams over the following year. These visits had a clear purpose, taking the form of development sessions combined with a notion of 'popping in' or keeping in contact to see how things were going and providing some support to the team manager. Equally important was external validation of the achievements by means of external inspection.

Our work with teams over the last two years has convinced us that positive change can happen if staff are fully included in the change process right from the beginning. Staff want to provide a safe and quality service for the children and families in their area. This is the reason they come to work. There are no quick fixes, however. It requires consistent and committed people who are supported by their organisation to carry out what is without doubt complex and often difficult work but work that can be so rewarding.

References

Balloch, S., McLean. J. and Fisher, M. (1999) *Social Services: Working Under Pressure.* London: Policy Press.

Burchell, D. (1992) 'Client Reception in Social Services Departments.' *Social Policy and Administration 26,* 4, 313–319.

Department of Health (2000) *A Quality Strategy for Social Care.* London: Department of Health.

Department of Health, Department for Education and Employment and the Home Office (2001) *Framework for the Assessment of Children in Need and their Families.* London: HMSO.

Hall, A.S. (1974) *The Point of Entry.* London: George Allen and Unwin.

Kanter, R.M., Stein, B.A. and Jick, T.D. (1992) *The Challenge of Organisational Change: How Companies Experience it and Leaders Guide it.* New York: Free Press.

Learner, E. and Rosen, G. (2001) *Duty First.* London: National Institute of Social Workers.

Marsh, P. and Fisher, M. (1992) *Good Intentions: Developing User-oriented Services Under the Children and Community Care Acts.* York: Joseph Rowntree Foundation.

National Task Force on Violence to Social Care Staff (2001) *A Safer Place.* www.doh.gov.uk/violencetaskforce.

CHAPTER 8

Managing Front Line Practice

Women and Men: The Social Care Workforce

Gayle Foster

Introduction

Supervision is concerned with the quartet of the service user, the carer, the practitioner and the first line manager. This quartet is set within the social context and the complex matrix of gender, strategic decision making and action. The concentration in this chapter is on women because they are the majority of the social care workforce. Many women managers, workers, service users and carers work tirelessly to mediate the poor effects of policies on themselves. They are not victims. They demonstrate an ingenuity, persistence, humour and practicality that demands celebration. The chapter begins by examining the gender structure of the social care workforce and the social context in which the quartet functions. It then moves to looking at the gendered nature of the problems women bring to social care workers. The final section examines gender and management styles, and first line management.

Gender and the workforce

> Social work and social care remain women's work, the majority of them having no formal qualifications. Practice continues to be undervalued while structures, procedures and management are over emphasised. (Hanmer and Statham 1999, p.5)

These assertions in the second edition of *Women and Social Work* continue to be true as major changes have taken place in national policies and legislation in social care and social work. Women are structurally located in less powerful positions as workers and as service users and carers. Strategic decision making takes place in a political context both locally and nationally that minimises the effects of policies on women. The emphasis on users' and carers' rights gives new and complex responsibilities to social service staff, and the aim is that the whole of the UK workforce should raise its skill levels and to remain up to date. Continuing professional development is no longer the preserve of the few. It is expected to be the norm. In spite of these radical changes gender issues are still frequently neglected in the supervision of front-line practice. This is no longer a viable stance. In the National Institute for Social Work (NISW) workforce survey of social work/social services departments, women constituted 86 per cent of the social care workforce, with men disproportionately represented in management (Balloch, Mclean and Fisher 1999).

In the UK workforce as a whole only 12 per cent of occupations in the UK have between 40 per cent and 60 per cent of men and women in them. When there is a minority gender in an occupation it tends to be in very small proportions and to be overrepresented in management positions. In the social care workforce gender distribution is at its most extreme in home care work where only 1 per cent of men were found in the NISW workforce survey (Balloch *et al.* 1999). The researchers also found that women workers tend to have fewer educational qualifications and are more likely to work part time. Ninety per cent of men had a formal educational qualification as opposed to 59 per cent of women, and among workers providing direct care to people using services 58 per cent had no educational qualifications compared with 24 per cent of the men.

Women and men from black and ethnic minority groups were underrepresented in management in the NISW survey, with 79 per cent in basic grade jobs compared with 62 per cent of white men. Nearly double the number of black and minority ethnic men were found in residential work, where almost twice as many white men were managers. The distribution of black and white women showed higher proportions of black women in residential and field work, whereas in home care there were only 28 per cent black women workers compared with 51 per cent of white women.

The implication is that if the aim is to raise the level of workers' qualifications there is a gender dimension to staff development and the role that supervision plays within the wider framework. Supervision offers the opportunity to individualise learning and to tailor it to the worker's own life, educational needs and career development.

Social care is concerned with providing personal support in the intimate areas of our lives whether physical, emotional or social. These are tasks in our society usually involving family, friends and workers who are frequently women. In the NISW workforce survey one-third of the workers were providing support to an adult member of their families. The work of providing personal and intimate support, whether as a family member, friend or worker, is often complex and combines the goals of facilitating empowerment and working with pain and distress, loss and change. There is little scrutiny of men's involvement in social care except as abusers (Hanmer and Statham 1999). In the same way that many women feel uncomfortable in the masculine cultures of senior management, men in all non-traditional occupations often have difficulties with coping with female work cultures and the lack of male companionship in the workplace (McLean 2002). The emphasis on integrated services, teamwork and practice which addresses outcomes that are defined by people using services means that the gendered experience of the worker is of crucial importance in the management of effective team and individual practice.

The social and economic context

It is useful to be reminded of the massive empirical evidence that

> women have lower wages than men even within the same occupation and at the same level, experience more unemployment than men, take more responsibility for unpaid labour, are strongly underrepresented at higher positions in working life, that they have less autonomy and control over work and lower expectations of promotion. (Alvesson and Due Billing 1997, p.1)

> Those arguing for the existence of a gender order or a patriarchy, which give many more options and privileges to men, particularly in working life but also in life in general, have no problems in substantiating their case. Clearly gender–patterned, socially produced, distinctions between female and male, feminine and masculine is a key concept for understanding what is happening in work…and life. (Alvesson and Due Billing 1997, p.1)

Women are the overwhelming majority of service users and carers, the overwhelming majority of social work and social care practitioners, and the majority of first line managers. The very pervasiveness of women may mean that issues, concerns and realities can be overlooked, trivialised or taken for granted. It may also be that their very numbers have led to a lack of differentiation between them, obscuring differences between them in terms of class, race, age, sexuality and abilities.

> Making women visible as service users, carers and workers involves a restructuring of thought and values: women must become valued in and for themselves. Making women visible also involves a greater understanding of the conflicts experienced by women and the demands made upon them, both as service users and as workers. It involves challenging current thinking about the way in which problems faced by women who use services are grouped together and about what is given priority. (Hammer and Statham 1999, p.11)

Women as service users and carers

Women are often carers and sometimes service users. In Chapter 5 a triangle between the social care worker, the service user and first-line managers is analysed as being key to good practice. This neatness has a conceptual appeal when the overwhelming responsibility of the legislation, and of the organisation, is focused on the service user, for example in cases of child abuse. More often the picture is more complicated and the interfaces that have to be managed are numerous. Carers who are family members or friends are almost always in the configuration, as are other professionals. It cannot be assumed that the interests of the service user and the carers are the same, or that they are completely divergent. Whether the management of practice is based on a trio, a quartet or more complicated configurations has a large impact on what can be and is achieved. Even the idea of a matrix or series of matrices may be too tidy a configuration to be useful in managing practice because it does not take into account gender.

For example: A very physically frail but mentally aware elderly woman in a hospital ward commits suicide after waiting many months to go home or to a residential establishment. What gender issues are imbedded in this bleak tale? Women are longer lived than men. Women find themselves old and frail, living on their own. Sometimes they have the help of family members, often other women. Sometimes they have the help of home care workers, district nurses, voluntary visitors, who usually are women. A health crisis, often a fall or illness leads to hospital admission. On hospital wards they are usually cared for by staff who are women. These frail elderly women may be or may become anxious, distressed and depressed about whether or not they can return home, whether they will go to a nursing home or to a residential home. How often would such women be considered for treatment for depression, for psychiatric assessment or for counselling? How would a mental health crisis be recognised? What assumptions are made by men and women staff about these women's needs, based on their gender and age? Would this suicide be seen as desperate depression or a success in reclaiming power and control? How often would these deaths among older people be recognised as suicide? A feminist analysis might argue for the overwhelming evidence of a male and ageist hegemony in which the majority of women have little power to influence the outcome for this woman, despite being the mediators of her treatment at virtually every point.

Women predominate as service users and carers because they are seen to be and very often are responsible primarily for caring for children, for the sick, for domestic tasks, for the elderly and disabled. This fact and the implications gender has for practice is obscured by the terms 'parent', 'service user' and 'carer'.

Domestic violence, gender and social care

Women and children are the victims of male violence and become the object of interventions to help and protect them. The ways in which domestic violence is identified and approached reflects the ways in which gender impacts on social care. There has been growth in the development of refuges for women and children, changes in reporting and police action in relation to violence against women and children. Men are more likely now than in the past to be charged, to appear in court and to be found guilty.

While provision has developed in relation to domestic violence, according to a mapping exercise on these services there is great unevenness in service provision across the UK. And, despite refuges diversifying to meet a range of needs of women and children, the survival of the work is continually threatened by lack of core funding in many areas (Humphreys and *et al.* 2000). Delivering a woman-centred service remains hard to sustain and a theoretical understanding of gender may be difficult to translate into practice unless developed and supported by guidelines and training.

Like many social care interventions the resource is focused on the victims of violence. And this is important and necessary work. What is not addressed is the simple fact that it is overwhelmingly men who assault women and children. Treatment directed at perpetrators of domestic violence is very limited and not very successful, although it may improve the balance of power in some domestic situations and so provide a small but significant improvement for some women and children. 'Programmes designed to prevent domestic violence do not always work, but they add to the sum of women's resources to fight domestic violence' (Campbell 2000, p.14).

What is missing is the core campaign that would address men and boys about violence and masculinity and attempt to break the link. Law-and-order rhetoric focuses on the public face of men's violence: public drunkenness, assault, threatening behaviour, robbery with violence, and so on. A focus on developing services and practice might be better aimed at addressing men's 'private' violent behaviour. A disturbing development has been the co-option of the 'zero tolerance' concept from the protection of women and children from men to unlawful behaviour generally and to the imposition of severe imprisonment penalties in response to the public violence. The idea has been co-opted to address a male problem, and this makes it difficult to use as a practice or campaign framework for women to protect themselves and each other.

Women and other areas of social care

There are many areas of practice where women become the focus for help or intervention, and many of these areas echo the issues raised above. For example, Sheppard (2000), writing about depression and child protection, encourages professionals to be aware of the prevalence of mothers suffering from clinical depression and how this may affect efforts to work with them (p.28–9). 'The depressed women frequently found it hard to summon the energy, motivation and confidence to engage in partnership' (Sheppard 2000).

While depression may be an important factor to consider in working with these mothers, there are also social, economic and gender factors which may have produced the clinical problems. To what extent were these women alone in their parenting responsibilities? Where were the fathers in this study? What clinical diagnosis applies to them? Working in partnership may be difficult or impossible in circumstances where the child protection professionals have power and skills that are not equalled by the mother in this relationship and which place her as an individual at the centre of the problem.

The media provide professionals as well as the public with an abbreviated and sometimes sensational view of social care policies and their impact. For example, the authority now exists for courts to order parents to attend parenting skills classes. This intervention is seen as supportive and educational rather than punitive in relation to assisting parents with troubled and troubling children. But the early evidence according to the media is that, although many parents do not attend the classes, those that do attend are predominately women.The recent sentencing of a woman to imprisonment for failing to ensure that her teenage daughters attended school ended with her accepting her responsibility for their non-attendance and promising to do better in the future.

An increasing proportion of women who offend are sentenced to imprisonment; this too reflects the ways in which law-and-order policies may have a disproportionate impact on women as well as others.

These examples illustrate the way in which society, social care organisations and women themselves expect women to take responsibility for circumstances over which they have little control. Further, efforts to assist or change these circumstances may further disempower women. New legislation, national initiatives, national guidelines for practice might benefit from considering women's positions and analysing the expected outcomes in relation to this as well as generating possible unexpected outcomes.

Men as service users

Men and women are service users in the whole range of social care. Men can be as vulnerable as women to poor service and practice. One area in which men seem to be more vulnerable to health and social care intervention that may be unhelpful is in mental health services. Young men are more likely to be subject to compulsory treatment orders under existing mental health legislation and practice. Young black men are much more likely to be diagnosed as schizophrenic than young men generally (Butt 1997). There are concerns that proposed changes in the Mental Health Acts in England and Wales, and Scotland, may lead to increased used of compulsory powers to ensure treatment in hospital or in the community.

Women as social workers and social care workers

> A very large part of the paid work women do today is allied to the traditional six tasks that women…(have in the past)…to care for children, the sick, the elderly, and the disabled, to clothe people, to be responsible for the education of children and to take care of the home. (Alvesson and Due Billing 1997, p.60)

Major change has taken place in home care services over the past twenty years: 'privatisation has depressed pay and conditions as the private sector pays lower wages and has less favourable terms of employment in general to local authorities' (*Community Care* 2000). At the same time, the proportion of direct public to independent provision is steadily reducing. Local authorities have adapted to changes that were in many ways undermining the most valuable features of the home care service. For example, new systems may undermine the way the care worker did their job in ways that users valued, being gentle and careful, cheerful and matter of fact, respectful of the user, sometimes disregarding departmental or agency guidance in order to meet the individual needs of the user. As we have seen in Chapter 2, flexibility, reliability, respect, putting the person first are the very things that gives a service its quality from the user perspective. A *Community Care* (2000) article that is full of useful information and good analysis never mentions that most home care is done by women, managed by women and provided to women.

> Most of the women social care workers and first line managers who attended a conference identified themselves as the primary carers for children, parents, aunts or uncles, or friends and neighbours. Almost one third of these, were in contact with their own or other social care organisations about the care of these family or friends.

The idea of a quartet for the management of practice rather than a trio provides a framework that links women service users, carers, social care workers and first line managers. Women in all these positions may be both workers and carers who come in contact with the formal service provision organisations.

> The competing demands of work and home significantly affect social care staff. A much higher proportion of social service staff were carers than in the general population in employment and their levels of stress were higher than for other staff. (Balloch *et al.* 1999, p.188)

This experience is more common among the social care work force than is recognised by employers or colleagues, and yet it is the backdrop of many women workers' lives. A number of examples are described and analysed which come from the author's experience as a consultant and social work colleague. For example:

> A woman team leader manages a team of social workers and social work assistants in providing community care assessments and care management to service users with physical disabilities. She has a family, a partner and children. Her parents live in another town, her mother has Alzheimer's Disease, and is looked after at home by her father and health and social care workers. She makes frequent trips to her parents, to check how things are going, to provide her father with a break, and to liaise with the services involved.

The failure to recognise gender as a key issue in practice and its management disadvantages women both as worker and service users.

Gender and management styles in social care

There has been an ongoing debate among management consultants and management researchers in the business and industry world about whether men and women manage differently. Some studies suggest that there are no significant differences in leadership styles or skills applied. Studies emphasised similarities, for example one study examined the behaviour of male and female managers in public administration in the USA and found that women and men varied only in relation to dedication to the job, women being more likely to take it more seriously and to work harder. Men and women did not manage using different leadership styles or in the views they expressed about the organisation (Alvesson and Due Billing 1997, p.143).

In another study of US women executives in the human services women identified themselves as managing differently from male colleagues. Their approach was categorised as '(a) concern for people, (b) sensitivity to the need of women workers, (c) investment in workers, (d) a co-operative orientation, (e) a global perspective, (f) openness in communication, (g) recognition of inequities, (h) concern for the quality of the environment, and (i) use of intuition' (Chernesky 1996, p.356). There seems to have been a wider acceptance that gender differences in management styles are real and a suggestion that women's style might be preferable. When a management guru like Tom Peters suggests this, it is taken seriously (Chernesky 1996). Differences that are perceived now between the management style of men and women may reflect too the socialisation of men and women and the internalised expectations each of has of how men and women should be.

The issue may be more complicated than whether men or women manage differently. For example, men and women may manage more similarly in relation to what is being managed, i.e., social care or business. It also likely that different styles of management are needed at different levels of the organisation and in relation to where and what is being managed in social care. Where you are in the structure of the organisation may make it more or less difficult to retain a gendered approach and a personal style. Similarly a home care organiser or residential home manager may need a different style and skills than a middle or senior manager. Whatever the answers to these questions gender remains an issue that has to be addressed in terms of practice and the life experience of social care workers.

Women as first line managers

First line managers have a key role in supporting, monitoring and developing social care practice. They will interpret organisational policies and procedures, legislative imperatives and practice standards to their teams. They will provide expertise and experience in risk assessment and management. And they will manage the workload of the team within stringent and sometimes difficult limits. They will be influential in supporting service user and carer empowerment or disempowerment, in developing work group morale or lack of it and in supporting and challenging team members' practice.

The majority of these managers are women: leaders of field social work teams, residential home managers, day care managers, home care organisers, occupational therapy team leaders and administrative team managers. A manager of a large retail UK company said:

> what I can't have is sixty very ambitious people as store managers. I only want ten very ambitious people. Fifty I see as being hard-core managers, permanent in the areas where they are. And what I am looking for, crudely, is thirty to forty year old females, with a good retail background, who are very effective and very efficient in their job but, because of their domestic circumstances, won't want to move. (Cockburn 1991, p.41, cited in Alvesson and DueBilling 1997)

This picture of women stuck in first line management in business contrasts with the evidence gathered by the author in her work with women first-line managers. For example, the women who took part in individual or group career development activities in a large English social services department welcomed the opportunity to reflect upon career decisions, describing a messy process of considering opportunity, interest, competence and life outside work and attempting to find a balance that suited each. Many of those who stayed in first line managers' posts did so from a wish to be close to practice, to develop good work and to support staff, and to balance this with their own and their families' interests and demands.

Women making or influencing strategic decisions in social work and social care

Women are underrepresented at senior levels given their predominance in the social work workforce. A 1997 local government management board figure showed that 84 per cent of the social services staff workforce in England and Wales were women. In the same year, of the 131 social services departments in England there were 26 women directors. There is still only one women director in Wales despite the increase in departments. The proportion of men to women directors did not change overall between 1992 and 1997. And while women have gained in some areas they have lost in others, for example in London social services departments.

There may be many reasons for the patterns and changes. Whatever the explanations, according to Joy Foster (1997) in a *Community Care* article, 'the patterns and processes of appointment at director level still point to discrimination again women and to a competition for appointments on playing fields which are far from level' (pp.19–20). The NISW research on workforce concluded that discrimination was not direct in relation to women reaching middle and senior management positions. The research showed the important differences between men and women were that women had shorter full-time service and a lower level of qualification (Balloch *et al.* 1999). This does not take into account the reasons that women find themselves in this position in the first place, and increasing the number of women in management positions continues to attract the attention of local and central government.

The Local Government Association launched its first gender equality strategy in November 2000. The strategy calls on local authorities to use the Best Value framework to achieve equal opportunities for all in four key areas: employment, representation, community involvement and access to services. Plans include use of Best Value indicators to set targets 'to increase the percentage of women in senior management in local government' (*Community Care* 2000). This is significant for more than cosmetic purposes. The life experiences of men and women continue to differ with only small changes in the redistribution of family and household responsibilities. Social care is about attention to the details of personal experience and focusing scarce resources on promoting as much control for the mostly women users as is possible. Men are in the majority in middle and senior management positions in social care, and they are likely to influential at national political, governmental and policy levels because they predominate in these positions of power. It is all too easy for the interests of women users, carers and workers to be lost as their gender becomes obscured in the neutered language of social care.

Gendered working in the service user, care worker, manager triangle

The framework of the quartet can help us look at whether there are any differences in the interactions between members of the quartet which help or hinder 'good' practice.

> Before the start of a discussion group, a woman home care organiser slices, butters and passes round rolls to other participants, while telling a colleague about staying late to take a canary into care because of an elder's sudden admission to hospital. She answers questions about her recent bout of illness, and talks about the stress she and others experience because of staff shortages. All at the same time, in a few short moments.

If a woman's way of managing is typical of what is described above, it is different from classical management notions of a linear approach to task achievement. It involves doing many things at once, acknowledging feelings, admitting vulnerabilities, recognising conflict, being both people and task centred, and being co-operative rather than competitive. If these ways are characteristic, they may help good practice. Social care depends upon the commitment of staff, particularly in home care, day and residential care. Staff work extra hours to meet the needs of service users, to cover the work of sick colleagues, to keep the service going. First line managers juggle organisational demands in order to meet the needs of staff and service users and carers. A key factor will be the extent to which the first-line manager recognises this commitment, supports workers, and listens to service users and carers.

> During a coffee break, a social work assistant tells of the death of a service user known to a few of the workers present. She is talked of with affection and admiration. A serious drug user, she developed remarkable shoplifting

skills, which she did not bother hiding from social workers. She gave up her drug use, got a flat, and succeeded in having her eldest daughter returned to her from care. These achievements were admired, too, and sadness expressed for her loss.

The NISW workforce research showed that social care workers were surprisingly satisfied with their work experiences. What the research did not reveal was some of the reasons for this. This may be with the uncertainty, drama, the challenge and level of risk associated with some service users' lives and what this contributes to those working with them. This satisfaction is particularly striking given the levels of stress and violence experienced by some workers.

The 12th Annual Social Service Workforce Survey commissioned by the Social and Health Care Workforce Group revealed that two-thirds of social services departments in England and Wales have difficulties with recruitment and retention of staff. There are shortages of mental health, child care particularly residential care staff. (Social and Health Care Workforce Group 2000)

The impact of legislation, local strategic decisions and practice procedures on women service users, workers and first line managers

The following discussion and examples provide an illustration of the impact of legislation, local decision making and practice in relation to the needs of frail or ill older women who come into contact with social care organisations. It would have been equally possible to offer examples in relation to learning disability or child abuse that would have made similar points. The way issues are structured profoundly influences how and what practice is managed. Where the focus is on rationing and there are limited conceptions of what older people need, practice solutions are produced that are equally limited: delaying raising eligibility criteria, applying complex administrative approaches to ration

An evaluation of the community care practice in a London Borough found that elderly women who were admitted to hospital and referred for a high level of community care often died before their comprehensive assessments had been completed, or before it had been implemented, or very soon after. (Foster and Barrett 1996)

The impact of the practice of community care on very frail, elderly people, who are mainly women, is the subject of much political and policy debate. The problem of bed blocking in acute hospital wards is blamed by hospital on social services, who in turn blame local and national funding systems for limited resources.

A social work colleague described how he has a template for community care summary and recommendations. This template is not simply an outline, instead its summary and recommendations are used over and over again, cut and pasted into reports because the arguments for residential or nursing home care are the same, whatever the individual's personality, social circumstances and needs.

The way in which complex community care assessment is structured, i.e., the guidance, and the paperwork surrounding the assessment seem to serve mainly to ration a scarce resource, either intensive packages of domiciliary care, or residential or nursing home care. It is difficult to see the benefit for women service users who suffer whatever illness or accident brought them to hospital, the indignity of blocking beds and the uncertainty of their future.

The management of practice should include using information that helps shape provision that addresses these aspects of women's lives. The predictability of death seems to have to be ignored by the planners, procedures and workers, although nurses and social workers 'know' the likely outcome. Women understand this and their vulnerability.

Among older women who have exceeded average life expectancy, quality of life is profoundly threatened by falls and hip fractures. Older women place a very high marginal value on their health. Any loss of ability to live independently in the community has a considerable detrimental effect on their quality of life. (Salkeld *et al.* 2000, p.341)

The rates of death of women over 85 in hospital are known, as is the outcome of assessment and care planning. This information could lead to a change in policy and practice. The government initiative to provide intermediate care for older people currently in acute hospital wards was developed jointly by health and social care. A positive outcome of intermediate care might be a period of convalescence and rehabilitation so that the older person could return home, if well managed. If not, the likely outcome may not be so positive and may lead to further disorientation, demoralisation and death.

There are a number of national initiatives that guide the ways in which statutory social care services develop and provide services. Quality Protects and Best Value are examples of these. They provide guidelines and resources for local social services and social work departments, and national standards for practice and services have been established, implemented and monitored. The Audit Commission and the Social Services Inspectorate aim to make the performance of statutory social care organisations more transparent and to insist that standards are observed or raised. Internal audits and inspections are now common and necessary. None the less, the criteria used for judging performance and the processes used to gather information and analyse performance are crude ones. They are not likely to reflect the messy, pragmatic, sometimes contradictory ways in which the social care worker, service user and carer interact, agree or disagree, and the ways in which the service user's wishes and needs are accommodated and the carer's needs and wishes, and the organisational imperatives, are met.

Further, the ways and the short time-scales in which policy initiatives are introduced, nationally and locally, may mean that the outcomes aimed for are not achieved. Some senior, middle and first line managers describe being bullied by their bosses and political representatives. This bullying becomes more than pressure to achieve difficult goals; it becomes hectoring that is demeaning and demoralising, and is experienced as personal, not occupational.

Conclusions

This chapter identifies a number of issues, provides information and examples, and invites the reader to consider the effect of gender on the workings of social care from her or his experience of it.

Gender is an important factor in social care. To recognise this is not to minimise other important factors such as race, age or class. Well-intentioned national policies and initiatives often ignore their impact and the unexpected consequences for women managers, social care workers, service users and carers. The aims of national standards of practice, and of departmental policies and procedures, may not be achieved if the messy, contradictory and changing situations of service users and carers, and those workers attempting to support and assist them, are not recognised in the management of practice.

However ingenious, persistent, humorous and practical service users, carers and workers are, they currently work in organisations and within systems which, while aiming to assist and support good practice, may actually do the opposite.

References

Alvesson, M. and Due Billing, Y. (1997) *Understanding Gender and Organisations.* London: Sage Publications.

Balloch, S., McLean, J. and Fisher, M. (1999) *Social Services: Working Under Pressure.* Bristol: Policy Press.

Butt, J. (1997) 'Race Equality.' *Research Matters*, April–October, 36–8.

Campbell, B. (2000) 'The limits of prevention.' *Community Care*, 26 October – 2 November, 14.

Chernesky, R. (1996) 'Women Managers are better: No they're not, Yes they are!' 11, 3, 356–61.

Community Care (2000) 'Comments.' 16–22 November, 21–2.

Foster, G. and Barrett, J. (1996) 'Evaluating Enfield Care Agencies' System of Assessment and Care Management.' *Social Services Research 4*, 1–7.

Foster, J. (1997) 'Management.' *Community Care*, 4–10 December, 19.

Hanmer, J. and Statham, D. (1999) *Women and Social Work: Towards a Women-centred Practice*, 2nd edn, British Association of Social Workers, London: Macmillan Press.

Humphreys, C., Hester, M., Hange, G., Mulluder, A., Abrahams, H. and Lowe, P. (2000) *From Good Intentions to Good Practice: Mapping Services Working with Families where there is Domestic Violence.* Bristol: Policy Press.

McLean, J. (2003) 'Men as Minority: Men employed in statutory social care work.' *Journal of Social Work 3*, 1, 45–68.

Salkeld, G., Cameron, I.D., Cumming, R.G., Easter, S., Seymour, J., Kurrle, S.E. Quine, S. (2000) 'Quality of Life Related to Fear of Falling and Hip Fracture in Older Women: A time trade off study.' *British Medical Journal 320*, 341–346.

Sheppard, M. (2000) 'The Depression Factor.' *Community Care*, 23–9 November, 28–9.

Social and Health Care Workforce Group (2000) *12th Annual Social Services Workforce Survey.* London: Employers' Organisation.

CHAPTER 9

Research and the Management of Practice

Daphne Statham

The relocation of the outcomes of practice from the periphery into the centre of policies requires a broader research agenda than in the past. Then the tendency was to examine different models of supervision and professional development, and methods of responding to individual and team learning needs. These areas remain an important component of the research agenda but are not sufficient to addresses the multitude of conditions and expectations of social work practice in the early twenty-first century. The chapters in this book have identified that that the management of practice includes:

- being a regulated profession within codes of conduct and standards for practice and services

- user-centred outcomes where the user, whether in the support or control aspects of the work, has been demonstrably involved

- holistic, and in consequence multidisciplinary and multiorganisational, practice to promote well-being

- the direct involvement of service users in the development of the organisation through contributing to policy, planning, practice, services, regulation and to education and training

- service users planning and running services themselves as individuals through direct payments and collectively through their organisations

- creating a culture in which a learning organisation can flourish and practice is informed by knowledge

- ensuring that there is a flow of information from front line for the purposes of governance and accountability and that policy and management information is used to shape the work of the team

- recognition that in specialist organisations for black and minority ethnic groups, for women, disability or gay groups, for example, discrimination and disadvantage will be experienced not only by individuals, families and communities, but by the workers and the organisation itself.

In addition degree-level qualifications for social work, continuing professional development and the work of SCIE all highlight the requirement for managers to be at a minimum research alert. Others will want to undertake research themselves. It is to be hoped that some will want to explore the management of practice, since it deserves no less research attention than other areas of social work practice. There is no dearth of areas including the following.

The impact of codes of practice, service standards and frameworks

Standards of service are now set at the national rather than the organisational level and codes of practice for social care staff and employers apply UK wide. These, backed by regulation and inspection, are a spur to the development and improvement of practice but we will not know for some time whether this will happen or how quickly. Gerrardine Cunningham in Chapter 5 shows that standards shape the content of supervision at the individual and team level, and feed into accountability and governance at the organisational level. They contribute to increasing the consistency between workers' practice and their assessments without regimenting these and provide the means for auditing practice and being accountable to people using services. The implementation of codes and standards and how they impact on outcomes for people using services need to be monitored to learn from this experience. There are likely to be differences in the support that needs to be in place between small, medium and large organisations that fulfil a multitude of purposes rather than having a single social work or social care focus. Other variables include where the worker's practice is open and visible, as in residential work, and where they are operating largely alone and unobserved in people's homes; and governance arrangements that range from politicians in local authorities to trustees in voluntary organisations and directors in private companies. Although all carry accountability for the quality of practice and services, how this is achieved will differ. We know less about the impact of these differences on the management of practice than we should when quality and good practice are closely identified with good outcomes for people using services. What works in these different structures to shift the organisation's focus on to practice? How is it sustained?

The social model and holistic practice

Embedded in the concept of good outcomes for people using services is a closer specification of what social work and social care can achieve and what resources have to be secured from organisations and workers that are outwith the control of the worker, the manager and their organisation. Joint planning and financing arrangements create formal and *ad hoc* arrangements providing a framework for multidisciplinary and multiagency working, but without practical daily working arrangements the experience of people using services do not change very much. Research on integrated health and social care teams found little difference in outcomes for service users. Patients referred themselves more quickly and received faster assessments. The improvements were in the effectiveness of the systems rather than in the outcomes. Integrated teams were having an impact on the process of service delivery, but there was little difference in other outcomes for service users. The exception was that more older people in the research sample than in the control group moved to residential homes. This was an unintended consequence and might have been the result of a dominance of the medical rather than the social model (Brown, Tucker and Domokos 2003). Levin *et al.*'s research found that the key to achieving better outcomes for older people in integrated primary care based teams was the relationship between the community nurse and the social worker. Given the complexity of the task in managing one dimension – that between health and social care – delivering holistic services is a key challenge for the management of practice. Learning from examples of practice that have achieved this, the skills, supports, the culture that enables it to flourish and survive, would provide a significant resource for managing front-line practice.

Working in partnership with people using services

Chapters 2 and 3 provide ample evidence that it is very difficult to implement the policy that people using services should be directly involved in identifying the outcomes they want for themselves as individuals and collectively. I never cease to be shocked by the consistent finding that service users do not think that social workers listen to them. Balloch and Taylor (2002) found that it tended to persist even when partnership was the specific objective of the relationship. Communication and active listening has been a major focus for education and training for many years and a central tenet of social work for as long as I can remember. Is this absence of active listening a defence against anxiety (Menzies Lyth 1988) or the dominance of 'the way it is done here' (Marsh and Fisher 1992)? Nicholas, Quereshi and Bamford (2003) suggest that the social model provides one of the tools to keep the focus on the outcomes service users want and suggest ways to achieve this. If we are to move away from the social worker covertly remaining the expert in other people's problems to a more open model of practice we need to understand what supports are necessary to enhance workers' capacity to listen, to communicate even when the news is bad, how to work alongside people in ways that recognise and value their expertise and experience.

Front line practitioners actively involved in the development of practice

Beresford, Croft and Wulff-Cochrane (Chapter 2) reported the shock that people using services felt when they learned how infrequently social workers were involved in developing practice at the national and organisational level. The workers themselves were the recipients of the results of the deliberation of others rather than active participants in developing practice. Their expertise and experience was too often not seen as a resource, and as a result the difficult task of translating policies into front line practice was missing. This takes more than a training course and has to be part of an ongoing process that addresses practitioners' issues and concerns as well as management imperatives to deliver. Nicolas *et al.* (2003) used the results of their research on promoting outcome-based practice to produce a training guide. They worked alongside practitioners as well as managers and service users to journey with them in order to understand what had to be in place for them to actively participate in outcomes-based practice. It was time consuming but led to a framework that could be implemented by front-line staff because they had been involved in its development. Work described in Chapter 5 on using standards in supervision and governance took some seven years to bed down. These approaches contrasts with the cry we often used to hear at NISW – 'Why didn't they ask us?' – when practitioners were faced with structures and frameworks that were not fit for purpose. Researchers who are committed to participatory or emancipatory models are well suited to charting and analysing the change journey undertaken by workers and service users to achieve practice improvements that address the messiness of practice and life as opposed to the neatness of policy.

Managing practice in different organisational structures

The dominant organisational form for social work has been the local authority, or large national or UK-wide voluntary organisations. Much less attention has been given to the existence of a minority of workers in community-based, specialist, black, disability, women's and gay groups or in the private sector or independent social work. Increasingly social workers will be found in user-controlled organisations. The structures within which social workers will be found in the future will diversify further as the number of multidisciplinary and multiagency teams and organisations increases. The impact of structure on the management of practice will come to the fore when the definition of a team is 'who ever is needed to accomplish the task' (Smale, Tuson and Statham 2000). When the team includes the service user, and often their family and members of their social network, as integral members of the team, this presents a very different management task since they are outwith the control of the manager. Holistic practice will most frequently require contributions from workers employed by other organisations similarly outwith the control of the manager. This is a very different context for the management of practice that needs further exploration as these models become the norm rather than the exception.

The Bibini Centre's (Chapter 4) practice is kept dynamic by the managers, staff and young people creating a space within which culturally competent practice flourishes at the same time as remaining engaged with their experience of racism and discrimination. This calls for expertise in demonstrating daily the acceptance of diversity and connectedness with the issues facing black and ethic minority families and communities in Manchester and structuring this experience so that the lessons learned are transferable more widely. This balance between creating a haven for practice to develop and at the same time remaining deeply embedded in the issues facing black children and young people and their communities is faced by women's groups, disability groups, gay groups and other specialist organisations. One of the ways they achieve this is through having a coherent philosophy and a clear mission that helps to hold this dual focus. In common with service-user-controlled organisations they see the life experience of the worker as a major resource in the development of services. This contrasts with mainstream organisations where life experience that connects with the life of people using their services is frequently seen as high risk and a sign of weakness in the worker (Turner and Evans, Chapter 3). Some 30 per cent of staff in local authorities are responsible for supporting an adult in their family (Balloch, McLean and Fisher 1999). The contrast in the way workers' own personal experience and expertise is regarded in these two approaches deserves attention.

Duty or intake teams within local authorities offer another example of a different style of managing practice (Learner and Rosen, Chapter 7). Their evidence is that more frequent interventions by the practice manager are necessary because of the rapid bombardment rate, the importance of accurate assessments of need and risks, and the time-scales involved. Similarly, Gerradine Cunningham in Chapter 5 raises the issues of social workers having line managers from other disciplines and how professional social work practice can be managed within these teams. The shift from a dominant model of employment for social workers in social service departments to greater diversity of employment patterns, together with the imperative for continuing professional development, raises issues about how this is to be achieved and the range of patterns for managing practice that are fit for purpose.

The role of the first line manager

Increased focus on the quality of practice at the front line as an indicator of organisational performance and on the perspective of people using services as a key component in assessing whether standards have been reached has highlighted the role of managing practice. Patricia Kearney (Chapter 6) sees first line managers as the mediators of standards. Their role is a complex and involves governance, holding the focus on outcomes valued by service users, auditing the needs for continuing professional development in their teams, contributing to that development, and providing and accessing management information. In multiprofessional teams they will have the skilful task of ensuring access to professional supervision where this lies outside their own area of expertise, and undertaking management of individuals and the team. There is little research on this role, the support needed to undertake it or specific training for it, or how this expertise in learning from and about practice could become a resource for training students. Many first line managers have undertaken a practice teachers award. This provides key skills in promoting learning from practice and conscious use of theories. It provides a sound foundation but is not focused on the specific management task. In specialist organisations there is in addition a heavy responsibility to manage the impact of the external environment on the lives of both staff and people using the services and on the organisation itself. With continuing professional development everyone in the organisation becomes a learner.

The learning organisation and the intelligent organisation

The imperative that organisations should use their own work as a resource for development, including learning from mistakes, again emphasises the importance of learning from and structuring front line experience. The issue for the organisation is how this information can be accessed and structured, and can contribute to developments. The standards and audit approach gave managers in the Ulster Community Trust a means of accessing information that gave managers a true knowledge of the state of practice. This knowledge is in files and in social workers' heads. It is also in the heads and experience of people using services and their organisations (Michael Turner and Clare Evans, Chapter 3; Peter Beresford, Suzy Croft and Elizabeth Wulff-Cochrane, Chapter 2). Patricia Kearney's (Chapter 6) view is that 'learning at work' is an evolving idea and requires greater exploration of 'the interplay between thinking and doing, learning from the work you do and how you do it'. For employers in all sectors and sizes of organisation it requires a radical change in the way they have operated. It means surfacing information and intelligence that is normally given low status in policy, service and organisational development. It requires not only that the individual learns how to learn but also embedding this within the way that the organisation routinely operates. The context in which this takes place is one of continuing change and multidisciplinary and multiorganisational working. It is a key area for research and development. The Kennedy Inquiry into child deaths at Bristol Infirmary prompted the Department of Health to review how organisations could learn from their own mistakes and what the aircraft industry calls 'near misses'. The term 'the intelligent organisation' was used to describe a culture within which this capacity could be developed. An exploration of how this culture could be achieved within social work would of necessity involve looking at practice management.

Conclusion

The management of practice is highly skilled and the context in which it is now operating places even greater emphasis on this expertise. Most of the chapters in this book are based on evaluation of developments undertaken either in the contributors' workplace or alongside teams as part of projects. All were based on reviews of the literature and substantial expertise and experience either as a service user or as a social worker. Each chapter raises questions that should be addressed through further research. We hope that this book is a spur to others to join this collective task and continue the journey of exploring the management of practice and its contribution to improving practice.

References

Balloch, S., Mclean, J. and Fisher, M. (1999) *Social Services: Working Under Pressure.* Bristol: Policy Press.

Balloch, S. and Taylor, M. (eds) (2002) *Partnership Working: Policy and Practice.* Bristol: Policy Press.

Brown, L., Tucker, C. and Domokos, T. (2003) 'Evaluating the Impact of Integrated Health and Social Care Teams on Older People Living in the Community.' In *Health and Social Care in the Community 11*, 2, 85–94.

Levin, E., Illiffe, S., Kharicha, K. and Davey, B. (2002) 'Research Across the Social and Primary Care Interface: Methodological issues and problems.' *Research Policy and Practice 20*, 3, 17–30.

Menzies Lyth, I. (1988) 'The Functioning of Social Defence Mechanisms as a Defence Against Anxiety.' In *Containing Anxiety in Institutions, Selected essays, Volume I.* London: Free Association Books.

Nicolas, E. Quereshi, H. and Bamford, C. (2003) *Outcomes into Practice: Focusing Practice and Information on the Outcomes People Value.* York: University of York Social Policy Research Unit.

Smale, G., Tuson, G. and Statham, D. (2000) *Social Work and Social Problems.* Basingstoke: Macmillan.

The Contributors

Peter Beresford is Professor of Social Policy and Director of the Centre for Citizen Participation at Brunel University. He is also a visiting fellow at the School of Social Work and Psychosocial Studies, University of East Anglia and Chair of Shaping Our Lives, a national user controlled organisation. He has had a longstanding involvement in the mental health services users/survivors movement and in issues of participation and empowerment as a writer, researcher, teacher and campaigner.

Suzy Croft is a specialist palliative care social worker at St John's Hospice London. She is also research fellow at the Centre for Citizen Participation, Brunel University and manages the Involve Research Project: What Service Users Want from Specialist Palliative Care Social Work. She is a member of the editorial collective of the Journal Critical Social Policy and has published widely in the field of participation.

Gerardine Cunningham has an honours degree in Social Anthropology from Queen's University. She entered social work in 1977 as a trainee social worker whilst training at Middlesex Polytechnic and has worked in Northern Ireland since qualifying. Her main area of interest is working with service users with Physical Disabilities. She now works in the Ulster Community and Hospitals Trust and is Programme Head for Physical and Sensory Disabilities. She also has responsibilities for social work education and training within the Trust.

Yoni Ejo was involved in the Black and In Care Group as a trustee for nearly five years. The group later became the Bibini Centre for black children and young people. Yoni was appointed as a manager and later became the Chief Executive of the next project. Yoni admits a strong and passionate commitment to the welfare of children. She is currently chairing child protection conferences within the local authority to enable her to adopt a little girl. Yoni lives in Manchester with her partner and three children.

Clare Evans is a disabled person who is a qualified social worker, practice teacher, lecturer, writer and researcher. She has published widely in how user involvement in social care can contribute to improving the life options of disabled people. She set up and directed the Wiltshire and Swindon Users' Network. This was one of the first examples of service users having a direct influence on the policies, services and culture of a local authority social services department. She is currently manager of the Leonard Cheshire Disabled People's Forum, a national initiative which is responsible for promoting the voices of disabled people and ensuring they have the peer support and training required to be effective.

Gayle Foster works as a social work practitioner with young people leaving care, and as a counsellor in primary care. She tends her gardens in Kent and Spain. She was a consultant with the NISW, with a wide experience of social work education and consultancy.

Patricia Kearney is currently Director of Practice Development at the Social Care Institute for Excellence. She read English at Somerville College, Oxford, and obtained a MSc in Applied Social Studies there in 1975. Her first job as a social worker was in an area office in Southwark Social Services Department. Since then she has worked as a social worker and a manager, as a social work teacher and trainer and in the Practice Development Unit of the National Institute of Social Work.

Eva Learner is a qualified social worker who has an extensive background as a practitioner, academic and manager, in Australia and the UK, often travelling between both countries. After beginning her career in hospital social work she moved into education and training in the UK and subsequently specialised in work with children and families. She was a member of the Lane Committee on the Working of the Abortion Act in GB,1971-74. Subsequently, during a period of work in Australia, she held a lectureship at La Trobe University where she also established the Human Resource Centre and was appointed as a (part time) Commissioner to the Victorian and N.S.W Law Reform Commissions. Since 1990 she has worked back in the UK, including a period as Head of Training for the National Association of CAB's, then working as an independent social worker. She has extensive experience of practice with high profile, complex child protection cases. Currently she is working in local authorities to improve practice standards where they have fallen below acceptable standards.

Gwen Rosen has worked in social care and social research since obtaining her qualification in social work in 1972. She has taught social work in universities in England and in North America. She has worked mainly in childcare as a manager and social worker in a variety of childcare settings. Her recent posts have included Director of the National Institute of Social Work and Sheffield University's MA

Programme in the Management of Social Care. She now works at the Social Care Institute for Excellence as a Project Manager on projects about learning organisations, front line manager development and service user involvement in SCIE. Her main interest is working with front line staff to develop the full potential of the team.

Daphne Statham is currently an honourary professor at the School of Health and Social Policy at Warwich University and works as part of a network of independent consultants called Practice Improvement Associates in authorities where practice has fallen below acceptable standards. She was previously Director of the National Institute for Social Work for 16 years prior to the transfer of most of its functions to the Social Care Institute for Excellence. Her career began in social work with children and families and moved into social work education and training during the mid 1960s. She has written widely on women and social work and on the future of social work. Her work on social work and social care education continues through Ruskin College, Oxford where she is an academic advisor, and her work on National Occupational Standards.

Michael Turner has been working in the disability movement for fifteen years. He worked extensively on social care services users' perspectives on outcomes for the Shaping Our Lives project from 1996-2002. The project led to the establishment of the Shaping Our Lives National Users Network in 2002. He is now Co-Director of the International Disability Equality Agency (IDEA) at the Centre for Social Action, De Montfort University.

Elizabeth Wulff-Cochrane is a qualified social worker who began her career in social work with children and families, and moved into social work education in the mid 1960s initially setting up and teaching on a qualifying programme for social workers. She worked at the Central Council for Education and Social work when it was set up in 1970 where she remained until the General Social Care Council took over CCETSW's responsibilities in 2001. Her career there focused on policy, research and development on practice and practice placements and residential care. Throughout her career she has championed the rights of people using services and of black and minority ethnic groups for ethnically sensitive practice, participation in education and training and in employment. It was in large part through her support that the work on the future of social work described in this chapter was possible.

Subject
Index

Author Index